THE WORKS OF JACQUES LACAN
An Introduction

THE WORKS OF
JACQUES LACAN

An Introduction

by
BICE BENVENUTO
and
ROGER KENNEDY

ST. MARTIN'S PRESS
New York

First published in the United States of America in 1986

Printed in Great Britain

ISBN 0-312-89015-X
ISBN 0-312-88956-9 (pbk.)

Library of Congress Cataloging-in-Publication Data
Benvenuto, Bice.
The works of Jacques Lacan.
Bibliography: p.
Includes index.
1. Lacan, Jacques, 1901- . 2. Psychoanalysis.
3. Imagery (Psychology) I. Kennedy, Roger.
II. Lacan, Jacques, 1901- . III. Title.
BF173.L15B46 1986 150.19'5'0924 86-3847
ISBN 0-312-89015-X
ISBN 0-312-88956-9 (pbk.)

Typeset by Rapidset and Design Ltd, London

Printed and bound by
Billings & Sons Ltd, Worcester

ACKNOWLEDGEMENTS

We would like to thank the following for permission to quote from published material:
Sigmund Freud Copyrights Ltd, The Institute of Psycho-Analysis and the Hogarth Press for permission to quote from the *Standard Edition of the Complete Psychological Works of Sigmund Freud*, translated and edited by James Strachey; Tavistock Publications for permission to quote from the English edition of Jacques Lacan's *Ecrits*, translated by Alan Sheridan; Mrs Richard Hunter for permission to quote from *Memoirs of My Nervous Illness* by Daniel Paul Schreber, translated by Ida Macalpine and Richard Hunter.

We would also like to thank Ann Scott for her expert editing, Bob Young of Free Association Books for his encouragement, and all of us would like to thank Elsie Buckenham for the quality of her typescript.

CONTENTS

Key to Abbreviations and Note on Ecrits

SE   Standard Edition of the Complete Psychological Works of Sigmund Freud, in 24 volumes, London, the Hogarth Press and The Institute of Psycho-Analysis, 1953-74.

E   Quotations from English translations of Lacan's *Ecrits*, by Alan Sheridan, London, Tavistock Publications, 1977.

E☆   Our modifications of Sheridan's translations, for which we alone are responsible.

e   Our translations direct from the French of Lacan's *Ecrits*, Paris, Editions du Seuil, 1966. No other English translation yet available.

Ecrits (1966)   French edition of Lacan's essays.

Ecrits (1977)   English translation of Lacan's essays by Alan Sheridan.

INTRODUCTION

THE AIM of this book is to give a clear introduction to the work of the French psychoanalyst Jacques Lacan. We present a historical exposition of his main ideas, following as far as possible their evolution and development. We think that this method of presentation will help the reader to follow Lacan's complex and elaborate thought more easily. We have begun with his doctoral thesis (1932) and have ended our exposition with one of his last major works, his seminar *Encore* (1972-3).

The task of writing an introduction to Lacan's work is far from easy. One should perhaps try to find a language and style that are both reasonably faithful to Lacan's thought, yet also English, and not some hybrid of French and English. We have not tried to imitate Lacan's unique French style, and although at times we have had to compromise on special terms and devise new, sometimes bizarre English equivalents, we do not offer these translations as final at all, and we are well aware of their limitations. Of course, we could also be criticized for castrating Lacan, and it may be said that the expression of his ideas without his style is like spaghetti without its sauce. There is obviously some truth in this assertion, and so in chapters 9 and 10 we have tried to use a rather more complex style, which attempts to capture some of the flavour of the original French. We have attempted this only after discussing Lacan's earlier ideas in ordinary English.

Where possible we have tried to put his ideas in a cultural and intellectual context. However, our main concern has been to present his ideas from a psychoanalytic perspective. We are aware of the limitations that this places on the book, but we think that a full consideration of the issues raised by Lacan's ideas for other disciplines is beyond our brief.

The first problem one encounters before making any assessment of Lacan as a psychoanalyst or as a general thinker is that of style. Lacan's work is divided into essays, most of which are in the collection *Ecrits* (1966), and seminars. The latter, which began in 1953 as a weekly meeting attended by, among others, analysts, linguists, philosophers and students, became the centre of his teaching after he broke with the French, and then later the international, psychoanalytic establishment. The style of the seminars is actually generally clear and fairly easy to follow, although it would be more true to describe them as lectures as there are only occasional interventions from the floor. The style of the essays, however, is far from easy to follow, and it is this fact that has invited considerable criticism both from within and from outside psychoanalytic circles. If one looks carefully, however, it can be seen that the prose style is not arbitrary. Whether or not one sympathizes with it, it has a purpose, which is intimately linked to Lacan's avowed intent – to re-interpret the work of Freud.

The so-called 'return to Freud' is at the heart of Lacan's work. Yet of course, most psychoanalysts consider that they are in some way or another returning to Freud, and it is uncommon to find a psychoanalytic paper without some reference to Freud. Each school of psychoanalysis considers that it has the correct interpretation of Freud's work. Indeed, for several years the British Institute of Psychoanalysis was deeply divided over Melanie Klein's re-interpretation of Freudian theory and practice, and it is only relatively recently that a truce has been called between Kleinians and Non-Kleinians. Thus the notion of a 'return' in itself is merely a slogan, and its basis needs to be examined. In order to do this, it helps to look at the history of psychoanalysis.

In Lacan's view, the innovative core of Freud's work belongs to the period that led up to the writing of *The Interpretation of Dreams* (1900) and continued to the papers on metapsychology, around 1915. During this period Freud laid out the detailed workings of the unconscious, with an excitement and intensity that do indeed seem relatively lacking in the later work. One can see this especially in *The Interpretation of Dreams*, which Freud considered the key to his discoveries, but also in the books that immediately followed – *The Psychopathology of Everyday Life* and *Jokes and their Relation to the Unconscious*. It was in them that the basic terms of psychoanalytic experience – the unconscious and sexuality – were first evolved and elaborated. The unconscious had existed as an idea long before Freud, but it was through the basic discoveries of psychoanalysis that the unconscious was seen to employ a specialized kind of language. The unconscious could then be understood as having a structure, and Freud could begin the task of formalizing his discoveries. Thus Lacan's 'return' generally consisted of a re-examination of the Freud of this innovative period. Lacan discussed Freud's later work many times but on the basis that the core of psychoanalysis was to be found in the earlier writings, and that Freud had deviated to some extent from the spirit of his early work. This approach to Freud is rather different from that of other psychoanalytic schools, which, at least until recently, generally accepted the early Freud, but felt that his later revisions were great improvements, and that the 'true' Freud was to be found in the work that used the later concepts of ego, id and super-ego. We outline these in chapter 2.

It would be too simplistic, however, to describe Lacan's 'return' as merely an emphasis on the early Freud for what he proposed was a particular reading of Freud's text. In

Lacan's view, all of Freud's work had been watered down and tamed, made socially acceptable and comfortable, by the analytical 'second generation' that followed Freud. The great and subversive discoveries had become deadened by routine use, while the training of analysts had become rigidly institutionalized and authoritarian. In addition, Freud's concepts had become virtually meaningless by an over-systematized and reductive interpretation of his writings. To deal with this unfortunate state of affairs and to restore psychoanalysis to life was Lacan's main purpose. To accomplish this task, he proposed a reading of Freud's text which would grasp the conflicts and 'knots' of his thought at their point of origin. In addition, Lacan evolved a style of writing whose aim was to avoid being over-systematized and reductive, and to reflect the workings of the unconscious. Lacan's prose thus often obeys the laws of the unconscious as they were formalized by Freud – it is full of puns, jokes, metaphors, irony and contradictions, and there are many similarities in its form to that of psychotic writing.

This makes reading his essays an intellectual task of some magnitude, on a par with reading *Finnegan's Wake*. As in that formidable work, there are innumerable references to literature and other disciplines, and one may often wonder whether ploughing through the book is worth the effort. Lacan himself was infuriatingly indifferent to such questions, for he maintained that one had to make a choice about whether or not one wanted to enter into his work. Of course, this is not a 'respectable' way of presenting oneself to serious commentators, and it must be admitted that such irreverence was typical of the man. To be fair to him, such a committing choice is basic to psychoanalysis and to the undertaking of a personal analysis. Such an uncompromising attitude was also typical of Freud. Unlike Lacan, however, Freud always took great care to make his presentation intelligible. Lacan also refused to define all his terms, and their meaning and function evolved over the years with little explanation. Indeed he was particularly interested in what cannot be limited to ordinary definitions: what comes out between the words for example; in speech, or between the lines, in the connections between words.

Such an approach is familiar to those who have experienced psychoanalysis, whether as analysts or analysands (patients), for the meaning in an analytic session tends to appear in these very roundabout ways, as slips of the tongue, dreams, jokes and puns. But what is unfamiliar is to use the very materials of the psychoanalytic session for so-called explanatory prose, and the result is often to produce a sense of bewilderment in the reader, for the ground seems to be taken from under his feet. Not unnaturally the reader then feels angry and resentful, and then that what he is reading is contemptible. It is perhaps partly for this reason that Lacan is often treated by readers, particularly in England and America, with a certain amount of contempt. One must say, however, that on the Continent Lacan continues to be a source of controversy but rarely an object of contempt, and he is taken seriously both as a psychoanalyst and as a major thinker. This difference in attitudes perhaps reflects some fundamental cultural difference between England and the Continent. First of all, the terms of thought are different – the philosophers Hegel, Heidegger and Husserl, for example, are considered on the Continent to be fundamentally important thinkers while here this is not so common, and they are sometimes attacked for unnecessary obscurity because of differences in presuppositions and preconceptions. Then the nature of the exchange of ideas is radically different – on the Continent there is much more cross-fertilization between different disciplines than here, where people tend to keep more to their own speciality. We are not necessarily saying that one culture is better than the other, but an appreciation of these differences may help to explain the apparent unacceptability of some of Lacan's ideas.

There are also major differences in the organization of

psychoanalysis, especially between France and England. The French situation could be described as chaotic, even more so since Lacan's death in 1981. There are several so-called 'official' psychoanalytic institutes, as well as various Lacanian organizations. At times, the organization of analytic practice seems as ordered as a heated conversation in a French café. In contrast, there is only one Institute of Psychoanalysis in London, which provides a professional, ordered, thorough but rather esoteric training, and which makes little contribution to cultural life. The British Society is also much more clinically oriented. Concepts are discussed, but mainly within a clinical context. This contrasts with Lacan's approach, and the French approach in general, in which clinical material only makes sense within a rigorous conceptual framework, or at least there is much more discussion of theoretical issues. One can detect this difference in Lacan's work, where there is hardly any reference to clinical material although, to be fair to the Lacanian school, followers such as Mannoni, Leclaire, and Safouan have attempted to make good this gap.

Through his uncompromising style, Lacan seemed in a very literal way to demonstrate how the traditional concept of reason was subverted by Freud, i.e., how Freud took the ground from under the concept of reason which had dominated western thought. He showed that the unconscious has its own laws, which are not those of conscious reason. The unconscious is, one might say, essentially subversive; it is organized in the form of a constant questioning of the human subject which cannot be limited and tamed by the laws of good common sense, however much people, including analysts and analytic institutions, may try.

Although one may quarrel with this literal attitude, as there is a danger that it may create a cult of the irrational, and it often seems doctrinaire, yet there are compensations. Through his rather 'Maoist' approach Lacan constantly challenged the terms and limits of psychoanalysis. For him psychoanalysis involves a constant dealing with its own limits, which are never pre-established once and for all.

This constant questioning of psychoanalysis is intended to open up issues that are normally covered by disciplines such as philosophy, natural science and anthropology. Indeed, one of Lacan's main concerns was the nature of the relationship between psychoanalysis and other disciplines. This concern included consideration of the problem of how psychoanalysis may carve out its own realm, as well as consideration of the status of psychoanalytic knowledge in relation to knowledge derived from other disciplines. It would thus seem important in any introduction to Lacan's thought to attempt to tackle his conceptions of the relationship between psychoanalysis and other disciplines, and to try to put his thought in some general context. However, we are also aware that our main task is to elucidate Lacan's thought, and in an introductory text this entails a certain amount of simplification.

As we shall see in chapter 4, one of the most important aspects of Lacan's revision of Freudian theory was his emphasis on the study of language. Lacan pointed out how often Freud referred to language, the proportion of analyses of language increasing when the unconscious was tackled directly. From the birth of analysis, language has been its primary field of action and the privileged instrument of its efficacy. Whereas Lacan pointed out that Freud did not have available to him the discoveries of modern linguistics, from the work of Saussure onwards, he did not go on to explain why Freud was ignorant of Saussure's work, in spite of having opportunities to become familiar with it. Saussure's posthumous *Course in General Linguistics*, compiled by his students from their lecture notes, was published in 1916, and Freud would have had plenty of opportunity to study the book. In addition, Raymond de Saussure, the linguist's son, became a psychoanalyst, and indeed Freud (SE19, p. 283) wrote a preface to Raymond de Saussure's *La méthode psychanalytique*, in 1922. Whatever the reason there was, Lacan claimed, a gap in Freud's linguistic formalizations, and he chose to remedy this gap by revising Freudian theory with the help of modern structural linguistics. But Lacan did not refer to the fact that there was considerable interest in linguistics and the concept of the unconscious, while Freud was making his early discoveries.

It is because of his debt to structural linguistics that Lacan has been loosely placed alongside those other French intellectuals such as Lévi-Strauss, Barthes, Foucault and Derrida, who have been categorized, rather inaccurately, as 'Structuralists'. It is probably inappropriate, for a variety of reasons, to lump all these thinkers together into one category. For example, each of them has original ideas, which one might lose sight of in such an arrangement. In addition, Foucault stated that he was not a Structuralist, while Derrida has consistently maintained a highly critical attitude to Structuralism. In addition, each thinker has resisted attempts to confine him within convenient cultural pigeonholes. Yet in spite of these considerations, all these thinkers have shared a similar cultural background; each has to a greater or lesser extent had a dialogue with structural linguistics; and they do have in common certain preoccupations, though from different perspectives. Such preoccupations include a study of the human 'subject', the nature of the 'speaking subject' and of meaning, the role of the 'text', and the function of signs.

Structuralism and Since (1979), edited by John Sturrock, which we draw on here, is a useful guide to the work of these thinkers, and provides a limited amount of comparison between them. Lacan may be distinguished from the others in various ways. First of all, he stated many times that his main concern was to talk to psychoanalysts about psychoanalysis, although he did not object if others were interested in what he had to say. It is for this reason that we approach Lacan in this book from the standpoint of psychoanalysis. This may create difficulties for readers who are not directly involved in psychoanalysis. We have tried to avoid being esoteric, without avoiding the fact that Lacan was first and foremost a psychoanalyst. Another feature which distinguished him from other thinkers was his approach to linguistics: he made a distinction between linguistics – the science concerned with the linguistic formalization of knowledge – and what he called La Linguisterie, which is concerned with the side of language that linguistics has left unformalized. La Linguisterie is the language with which the unconscious is concerned, and which psychoanalysis grasps at the moments of failure of language itself; when meaning fails, stumbles, or falls to pieces. La Linguisterie is, as it were, the science of the word that fails, and thus Lacan was concerned with what one could call the 'margins' of ordinary language.

Lacan's work seems to have a dual attraction – on the one hand it expresses, as a literary performance, the disintegration of language, while at the same time it offers the prospect of a solution to the 'lack' that it expresses. Solutions are very seductive, and at the same time dangerous. Anyone who says with enough conviction and charisma that he has *the* interpretation of Freud, or the right approach to questioning the human subject, could be expected to attract a following. It seems hard at times to sort out Lacan's original ideas from the polemics he used against those who disagreed with him; but then he shared this dilemma with Freud. Indeed, from its inception, psychoanalysis has been unable to free itself totally from the prejudices and illusions that belong to religion. The vigour and rancour with which Freud, Lacan, Klein and others have defended their positions merely reminds one that psychoanalysis deals with the human passions, and that analysts are no more free from passion than their patients.

The orthodox assumption is that at least the analyst is supposed to know what he is doing, when he analyses, yet Lacan pitched many of his interventions at precisely this assumption about the analyst's knowledge. He was particularly concerned with the status of the knowledge with which the psychoanalyst deals, and for him, psychoanalysis is based on a fundamental split between the subject and the knowledge he has of himself. Psychoanalysis deals particularly with wishes and desires that are unknown to the subject, and appear only in the unconscious. As we will explain in more detail, this position implies a radical revision of the concept of the human subject. The subject is no longer, as in traditional psychology, a unified collection of thoughts and feelings, but is 'de-centred', marked by an essential split. Throughout Lacan's work there are innumerable references to this new concept of the subject, described as 'lacking', 'fading', 'alienated', marked by an essential 'lack of being', 'split', possessed of an 'empty centre' (béance), etc.

Lacan was insistent that this notion of the human subject was essentially that of Freud, who, in his view, did not agree to a notion of the 'unity' of the subject except as a phantasy, e.g., the infant's phantasy of being one with the mother. This is certainly not the opinion of other schools of psychoanalysis, most of whom make space for some unifying concept of 'self'. We incline to Lacan's view, but the issue would seem to be one of differing interpretations of Freud's text, which is far from clear on this point, perhaps because Freud was struggling with new concepts while still in debt to the older language of nineteenth century determination.

Whatever one's interpretation of the concept of the human subject, at least Lacan has opened up an important area for discussion, with relevance to disciplines other than psychoanalysis. In addition, it would seem to be more sensible to examine this view of the human subject in its own right – regardless of whether or not Freud thought that way – so long as one is very careful about terms, which can often be confusing.

We will now outline the plan of the book, and some of the main themes of each chapter. For convenience we have divided up Lacan's work into three periods, represented in the book by three sections, in each of which we have discussed a selection of his major works. Our choice of material for presentation and discussion is somewhat restricted, as we have attempted to consider Lacan's main texts, or ones representative of his main areas of achievement and interest, and where possible those that have been translated into English.

The first period extends from his early neurological papers and doctoral thesis (1932) to his break with the psychoanalytic establishment, and ends with the presentation in Rome of his address 'The function and field of speech and language in psychoanalysis' (1953), commonly known as the Rome Discourse.

In chapter 1 we give a detailed account of the major themes of his thesis, which was on the relation between paranoid psychosis and the personality. Although an academic work addressed to traditional psychiatry, the thesis also marked Lacan's break with it and his entry into psychoanalysis. We thought it worthwhile to present the thesis in some detail, as it was Lacan's only detailed case history. However, one must say that it is not the record of a psychoanalytic treatment. One can detect his dissatisfaction with the limits of traditional psychiatry, and see how he tried to fit Freud into the clinical picture, but he was still confined within psychiatric parameters. Thus one has no account of individual sessions, and little interpretation of detailed clinical material, such as one can readily see in Freud's case studies. On the other hand, the move from psychiatry to psychoanalysis is a common one for those who find psychiatry intellectually limiting and emotionally deadening, and one can see in the thesis an attempt to acknowledge the individuality and complexity of the human subject. It marks an important moment of transition in Lacan's intellectual biography.

In chapter 2 we present Lacan's first major psychoanalytic contribution – his formulation of the 'mirror stage' (1936), a theme running through all his work and drawn from the observation of infants perceiving their own reflection in a mirror. In Lacan's words, the 'helpless' infant, not yet objectively in control of his movements, jubilantly perceives in the mirror – in an imaginary plane – the mastery of his bodily unity, which objectively he still lacks. The infant becomes aware, through seeing his image in the mirror, of his own body as a totality, as a total form or *Gestalt*. Lacan pointed to the difference between the infant's objective state of fragmentation and insufficiency, and the illusory feeling of autonomy and unity experienced as a result of seeing his own image in the mirror. The concept of the mirror phase went beyond child psychology, and became the core of Lacan's theory of the human subject, in which all notions of unity and absolute autonomy were swept aside as mere illusions.

Chapter 3 is a discussion of Lacan's paper 'Beyond the reality principle' (1936). This paper, which seems fundamental to much of Lacan's later work, tackles the different issue of the relationship between science and psychoanalysis, and whether the latter can claim its own realm of knowledge independent of the positive sciences. This represents a particular interpretation of Freud. Lacan took the view that Freud was moving away from the methodology of the natural sciences; but it can be argued that Freud himself was uneasy about this move. Freud wanted to be scientific, yet he was also aware that his discoveries veered away from the assumptions of natural science. Lacan seems to be quite clear that Freud was moving into the area of what are now called the 'human sciences', those disciplines essentially concerned with human meaning. This is certainly a valid interpretation of Freud's position, and is shared by many analysts; it contrasts, however, with the view of the American ego psychology school, founded by Heinz Hartmann, one of the many Central European analysts who emigrated to the USA before World War Two, who tried to incorporate traditional psychological thinking into psychoanalysis. The dialogue between those analysts who favour a natural science approach, and those who follow Lacan's line continues to this day. However, Lacan was clear where his allegiances lay, and his attack on traditional psychology remained the basis for his theory of the human subject.

The second period extends from 1953 to the late fifties, and involves a continuous development, both of the ideas put forward in the Rome Discourse and of earlier ones.

In chapter 4 we give a bare outline of the long Rome Discourse, a report given to the Congrès des psychanalystes de langue française in Rome, September 1953. With this address, and the beginning of his widely attended weekly seminar, Lacan introduced his study of language into his approach to psychoanalysis. As vice-president of the Paris psychoanalytic society, Lacan had been asked to deliver a theoretical report in Rome. At that time however there were serious disagreements within the Paris society which finally led to a split, just before the congress. Daniel Lagache, soon joined by Lacan, founded a new Société française de psychanalyse in June 1953, but it never acquired full recognition by the official International Psychoanalytic Association (IPA).

The secession was caused by a number of factors. Lacan and his followers felt that the Paris society had become impossibly rigid and authoritarian. They attacked its teaching methods, which took little account of the independence of the students. At the same time Lacan himself was attacked for both his uncompromising attitude and his analytic practice. The usual analytic session lasts 50 minutes, with only the very occasional deviation, and Lacan had introduced short sessions, the length of time being determined by the analyst. This clearly seemed a major breach of analytic practice, and one that could undermine the status of the discipline. In particular, it seemed to give the analyst an unprecedented omnipotence – he was the one who would somehow know what should be the right length of the session. The International Association debated Lacan's right to remain an officially recognized analyst for some years, and finally expelled him from the IPA in 1963, using his unorthodox analytic practice as the main reason.

In the debate, however, some of the valid points of Lacan's practice were missed. Experiments with the length of the session had often been carried out in the early days of psychoanalysis, particularly by Ferenczi, with some success. Also, Lacan was trying to point out that one has to question the meaning given to the termination of the session; a rigid insistence on maintaining a standard length in every session might interrupt the whole movement of the patient's discourse. His point has some validity; one must say, however, that the rigidity of the analytic session is an enormous protection for the patient.

The secession resulted in Lacan's becoming the centre of a new and influential psychoanalytic movement. Teaching was organized around the weekly seminar, which gradually became almost an institution, and thinkers from many fields attended it at one time or another. One may legitimately quarrel with the high-handed way Lacan often treated his opponents, but he was personally responsible for the revitalization of French psychoanalysis. However much they have tried, no analysts in France have been able to escape his influence, and his intellect and personality tower over them. Until 1966, Lacan was known to French intellectuals; but in that year, his *Ecrits* were published, and then began the explosion of his influence in French society. He became not only someone who questioned the meaning of culture, but also what one could call a 'cultural phenomenon'.

The Rome Discourse is, in a way, a blueprint for Lacan's whole future career. It was given in the context of great controversy, it addressed itself to a radical re-examination of the status of psychoanalysis, and it was written in the dense, contorted and many-layered style that became his trademark. It also moves freely from one topic to another; using ideas and references from several other disciplines. This easy flowing from one thinker to another, from Freud to Aristotle, from Spinoza to Saussure, is intellectually exciting, as is the way Lacan restored Freud's insights to life by re-examining their foundations. He wanted, he said, to provide analysts with a 'solid support for their labours'. He wanted a 'proper return to a field in which the analyst ought to be past master: the study of the functions of speech'.

In chapter 5, we discuss Lacan's 1956 essay on Edgar Allan Poe's short story 'The Purloined Letter'. This essay was placed at the head of the *Ecrits* (1966), perhaps for several reasons. Lacan used the story to illustrate and develop several of his basic themes; but the story itself, when given a psychoanalytic reading, seems to become a fable of the analytic process. Of course, the use of literature both to illustrate psychoanalytic themes and as a source of insights that psychoanalysis can use was a technique Freud often employed. But there seems to be an additional message in the Lacan essay. It consists of a psychoanalytic reading of a text, yet it seems to be saying at the outset that Lacan's text too is to be read in a particular way. Thus the essay represents both what will follow it, and establishes the mode of reading it.

The subject of the story is a letter, and Lacan traced the effect on the characters as it changes hands and follows a complicated path, its route and displacements determining the action and destiny of the characters. Like a signifier (or sound-image, a term which we explain in Appendix 1 on Linguistics), the letter travels in a definite path, forming a symbolic circuit which cuts across the subjects of the story. In order to read Lacan, the story seems to be saying, one must follow the path of the signifier, and the remainder of

Ecrits is fundamentally concerned with the laws of the signifier.

Lacan's important 1957 paper, 'The instance of the letter, or reason since Freud', outlined in chapter 6, tackles many of the details of these laws as Lacan understood them. It is concerned particularly with his own interpretation of Saussure's concept of the sign. Saussure conceived of the sign as made up of two inextricably linked elements – the signified (concept) and the signifier (sound-image). But Lacan saw the signified and signifier as two distinct and separate elements in a radical opposition, and he gave a new emphasis to the bar between them. It became a formula of separateness, rather than of the reciprocity between signifier and signified.

If one agrees with this new interpretation, then a number of important consequences follow. Lacan placed the signified *under* the signifier, symbolically emphasizing the primacy of the signifier. In this scheme, it is vain to search for the signified, or the concept. The signified is always slipping out of reach, and resists attempts to keep it fixed. What *is* available, however, is the signifier. It is revealed in the signifying chain, which is made up of signifiers connected to one another, and it is the analyst's task to uncover the many and varied relationships between signifiers. Meaning is produced in the very connections; from this would follow a new way of interpreting clinical material, including dreams. More attention is given to the details of the dream, to the individual items recounted, to the details of the 'manifest' content, while less emphasis is given to the pursuit of a mysterious signified that lies hidden somewhere. Presumably this does not at all mean that one forgets the analysand's associations, but rather that they are given a different kind of interpretation.

The reversal of the Saussurian sign has more than simply clinical relevance. If it is right so to reverse it, then all our notions of knowledge are turned upside down. Gone is the never-ending quest for the concept as such. Instead one is left with the available signifier, whose laws must be followed if one is to uncover knowledge about the subject. This new emphasis certainly makes sense in a psychoanalytic context, and one could interpret Freud's early work as a kind of quest for the rules of the signifier at play. But whether or not one could apply these ideas beyond psychoanalysis is more debatable.

Chapter 6 also deals with the concepts of metaphor and metonymy. We explain how reading Lacan's texts is like analytic work, where one has to follow the meaning as it gradually unfolds itself. That is, one is following not only the usual rules of grammar and writing, but in addition, or often instead, the way that one metaphor leads to another, or what takes place in the connections between words (metonymy).

Chapter 7 gives a relatively schematized account of the Oedipus complex through the Lacanian perspective. It seemed important to us to expound some direct clinical implications of Lacan's work, and we have included an account of Lacan's interpretation of Freud's case history 'Little Hans', which involves a study of the role of the signifier in clinical material. We describe how the resolution of Hans' phobia occurred by means of a transformation and permutation of signifiers. Although by no means the only way of interpreting this case history, Lacan's approach sheds new light on the concept of castration and the workings of the Oedipus complex.

In chapter 8 we discuss Lacan's ideas on psychosis, mainly from a clinical point of view. His first published papers concerned psychotic patients, and his thesis discussed paranoid psychosis, but comments on psychosis are also scattered throughout his works. We have tried to bring together the most significant of these ideas, based mainly on his essay on psychosis (1957-8).

Lacan's theories on psychosis are perhaps among the least controversial and the most easily acceptable of all his writ-

THE WORKS OF JACQUES LACAN

ings. They are based on a close reading of Freud, as well as the application of Saussurian linguistics, but within a very clear clinical context, which makes them particularly available to the English reader.

The third period extends from 1960 until Lacan's death in 1981. In 1964 Lacan reformed his analytic society, calling it L'Ecole Freudienne de Paris. But in 1980 he dissolved the school, and created a new society called La Cause Freudienne. Not surprisingly, this latter move created an enormous uproar, especially when Lacan proposed to make use of the money from the Ecole Freudienne. It is still difficult to sort out what happened, and to understand the motives. Lacan seemed to feel that the Ecole Freudienne was becoming too institutionalized, that it ought to be dissolved, and that several analysts ought to be refused admission to the new society. Lacan's authority to do this himself, without consultation, was questioned, and he was taken to court. His defenders claimed that *he* was the Ecole Freudienne, and so he could do what he liked, while his critics were incensed by his behaviour.

Rumours about Lacan's mental state abounded; but his seminar continued, and there is no evidence from the published text that he was in any way different then than before the crisis. The overturning of the Ecole Freudienne seems totally consistent with the unorthodox way he had treated all institutional questions. His death came before the legal battle was sorted out, and in the aftermath of both, the French psychoanalytic scene seemed as chaotic as ever, although there are some signs that analysts from various organizations are trying to come together now that Le Maître has gone, as we describe in the final chapter.

Chapters 9 and 10 deal with some of the basic ideas of the third period of Lacan's work. Chapter 9 deals with Lacan's later theory of the human subject, which argued that the dominance of the signifier subverts traditional theories of the human subject. We also discuss the Lacanian concept of lack, which is important for his account of the Oedipus complex and the nature of desire. The chapter enlarges on several themes from the previous chapters, but in a somewhat wider perspective, touching on philosophical issues raised by psychoanalysis.

Chapter 10 deals with feminine sexuality, the subject of his 1972-3 seminar *Encore*. We have ended our exposition with a discussion of this text because it was perhaps Lacan's last major work; it is currently, in France, one of the most widely debated of his works; and it deals with several issues, particularly the nature of the Oedipus complex, in a new perspective. Lacan himself felt that, with his consideration of feminine sexuality, he was coming up against the current limits and enigmas of psychoanalysis, which if successfully negotiated might open up new ground for investigation. Thus this work seemed, more than any other, to be definitely aimed at the future, and so it is suitable to end the exposition with it.

Chapter 11 is a summary of the main points of the book, including a short account of recent developments in Lacanian psychoanalysis.

It is the aim of the book not only to explain Lacan's major theories, but also to underline his main contributions to psychoanalysis: first and foremost his attempt to restore psychoanalysis to life by a radical return to the writings of Freud, and by putting psychoanalysis in touch with the latest developments in contemporary thought.

I

CHAPTER ONE

FIRST WORKS
(1926–1933)

L ACAN'S first articles were published between 1926 and 1933 while he was training as a psychiatrist. Most of them were written in collaboration with other authors, and were on neurological and psychiatric topics. They culminated in his major work of this period, his doctoral thesis 'Paranoid psychosis and its relation to the personality' (1932), which was based on observations of several patients, but which concentrated on the details of one female psychotic, whom he called Aimée.

Some of these early papers were pure neurology, on Parkinsonism, neurosyphilis and eye-movement abnormalities; two were on hysteria; and several were concerned with the organic features of various mental disorders, and were consistent with orthodox psychiatric thought. It is in Lacan's first publication as sole author ('Structure of paranoid psychoses', 1931a) that one can see the beginnings of an original contribution and hints of later preoccupations with structure and language. He wrote, for example, that progress in psychiatry would be made by studying the 'mental' structures' common to different clinical syndromes, and that an analysis of these structures was indispensable to classification of mental disorders, and would also be valuable in assessing prognosis and treatment. He wrote that he had formed this opinion as a result of his studies of patients suffering from delusions. He was particularly interested in their disorders of language, and in applying linguistic methods to the understanding of the written manifestations of delusional language. He added that his research had convinced him that no psychical phenomenon could arise completely independently of the subject's personality. This attitude is basic to psychoanalytic thinking, which Lacan was soon to embrace, and contrasts with most psychiatric opinion, which to this day maintains that psychotic phenomena cannot be understood in terms of the previous personality of the subject, but arise instead as a result of an organic 'process' or illness, e.g., some as yet undiscovered biochemical lesion which produces the symptoms automatically, for example by causing some kind of brain damage.

Lacan elaborated a number of these ideas in the thesis (1932, p.351) which is of interest for several reasons. Although often couched in academic language, and owing much to his teachers and to contemporary psychiatry, particularly in Germany, it contained some original ideas which laid the basis for his subsequent work and to which he returned. While not a psychoanalyst, Lacan used some analytic concepts in his account of his patient Aimée at a time when Freud was not well-known in France. He also raised issues which are still being debated about the nature of mental disorders.

One should perhaps stress how difficult it was at this time, in France, to take a serious interest in psychoanalysis. Indeed, it seemed to be a somewhat subversive topic. This resistance to psychoanalysis in France forms one important backdrop to Lacan's early career, and perhaps helps to understand not only his later 'subversive' approach to psychoanalysis, but also much of the 'missionary zeal' with which he approached the dissemination of analytic ideas.

Lacan's intention in the thesis was to show that his patient's psychosis could be understood as the reaction of her personality to events in her life, and involved conflicts within her personality. The case study demonstrated the purely psychological sources of the psychosis: that is, that it had a psychological meaning which involved intelligible connections between her psychotic symptoms and the events of her life, and that these psychological sources were enough to explain the psychosis. Such an approach had already been developed by a few German psychiatrists, notably Bleuler and Kretschmer, and of course Freud; by Meyer in America; and to some extent by Janet in France. But it seems that Lacan's thesis was the first French attempt to interpret a psychosis in terms of the total history of the patient – that is, by bringing to light as much detail as possible about her background, including her conscious and unconscious intentions. The thesis included a selection of Aimée's copious writings, which were produced at the height of her psychosis, and virtually stopped when it abated.

The literary qualities of Aimée's work were appreciated and discussed by members of the surrealist movement, and Lacan's connections with the surrealist movement form another important key to understanding his early and subsequent career. Aimée was not only a patient of Lacan's, but was also a *cause célèbre* for the surrealists. Lacan wrote articles for the surrealist magazine *Minotaure*, one of which concerned the case of the murderous Papin sisters (the case apparently formed the basis for Genet's play *The Maids*). Lacan's subsequent anti-establishment attitude, his talent for abuse, as well as his poetic voice, owe much to the surrealist movement. Surrealism's overturning of the place of conscious reason, its questioning of the reality of the object, its cultivation of the absurd, and its emphasis on the omnipotence of desire, do seem to have provided Lacan with many of his basic attitudes. However, it would not be true to state that he produced automatic writing in the surrealist mould. On the contrary, his writing has always born the marks of considerable elaboration.

After an introduction, Lacan discussed the concept of personality, and ultimately put forward his own notion, which was based on three parameters: the subject's history, his image of himself, and his social relations. This notion implied firstly, that the subject had a comprehensible psychological development in time, a 'lived history', which followed a definite pattern and was based on structures common to everyone; secondly, that the subject had a consciousness of himself as someone who thought, spoke and had intentions. This also included the more or less 'ideal' images that he had of himself; and thirdly, that the subject was not isolated but was affected by others, and his conduct and values were influenced by them. This fact could produce various tensions and conflicts between the subject and others.

Lacan then reviewed in great detail contemporary ideas on the aetiology of paranoid psychosis, comparing psychiatrists like himself, who considered that – with the exception of psychoses with obvious organic causes, such as severe drug abuse – they could be explained as reactions of the personality; with psychiatrists who thought that they were determined by an organic process. It may be said that a fair proportion of psychiatrists now hold a middle view. Lacan also discussed the possible contributions of organic causes in general, rejecting them as non-essential in the case of Aimée.

Next, he gave the details of Aimée's case history. We have had to piece together the details of the case from different parts of the thesis as his presentation was detailed and complex, interweaving the various aspects of Aimée's personality and her psychotic reactions.

Aimée was admitted to a mental hospital after attacking and wounding a well-known Parisian actress, whom she did not know personally, with a knife. When questioned by the police she said that this actress had been spreading scandal about her, and was also associated with a certain famous writer who had supposedly revealed many details of Aimée's private life in a book. Aimée was clearly suffering from delusions of being persecuted, which in fact cleared up three

34

weeks after her internment in prison, though she stayed a further eighteen months in hospital, where Lacan obtained the details of her history.

Aimée was 38 years old on admission, and had been separated from her husband, who had custody of their son, for six years. She came from a village family, with three younger brothers and two older sisters, and had had regular work in the administration of a railway company from the age of eighteen. Her father appeared rather tyrannical, but Aimée was the only one to stand up to him, and to his constant criticisms of her appearance and dress. Aimée and her mother had a close and intense relationship, and when talking about her Aimée would often break into tears, repeatedly saying that she should never have left her and that they were like two friends. The mother appeared to suffer from delusions of being persecuted by the neighbours, whom she blamed for her daughter's problems. While the mother was pregnant with Aimée her eldest child died tragically, in front of her eyes – she fell into an open furnace and expired from severe burns.

Aimée was particularly fond of playing with her brothers and was rather a tomboy, although her eldest sister did have a large, even dominant influence on her in childhood (and in her later life, as we shall see). She had a great love of nature, and used to enjoy solitary day-dreaming in the countryside; these intense reveries seemed to be indicative of a fertile and expansive, though rather precarious, imaginative life. Two episodes when she was an adolescent deeply affected her and later inspired pieces of writing: the first was the death from tuberculosis of a close girlfriend. The second was described by the family as typical of Aimée's behaviour. The family was going out, but she had spent so long on preparing herself that the others left without her. She went to join them by crossing a field, but had the misfortune to irritate a bull from which she just managed to escape. The theme of the pursuing bull often returned in her dreams and writings as an evil omen.

Aimée's first love affair took place in her early twenties in a small town, with the local 'Don Juan'. After seducing her one month before she left, he admitted that she was merely the object of a bet. Nonetheless, for three years and while living in another town, she continued to dream of an ideal liaison with him and was constantly occupied with totally unrealistic thoughts about him. She was frigid in her subsequent sexual encounters. When she moved to the Paris region her tormentor suddenly, for no obvious reason, became the object of her hate and scorn. This sudden change of love to hate seemed typical of her personality, as we shall see.

For four years, until her marriage, Aimée had an intimate friendship with a female colleague from work who was her complete opposite. The woman came from an aristocratic family fallen on hard times and felt that the work she was forced to do was inferior to her station; so she spent her time trying to impose her moral and intellectual leadership on the small world of her colleagues. She was also a great organizer of soirées, where conversation and bridge games continued well into the night. It was from her friend that Aimée learned the name of the actress she later stabbed, for this actress was the neighbour of the friend's aunt, and of Sarah Bernhardt, whom the friend's mother knew at convent school. The two actresses later became Aimée's major persecutors.

Aimée and her friend grew intimate. Aimée lived in her shadow, delighting in the fact that she was the only person she, Aimée, knew who was 'a bit out of the ordinary'. However, encouraged by her friend, she reacted with constant hostility to colleagues, especially the women, whom she despised as petty and silly, though she was clearly also jealous of them. She began to feel that she was masculine and was very attracted by masculine characteristics; but after a series of unsatisfactory affairs with men, she married a colleague who seemed a fairly down-to-earth and secure person, though not particularly sensitive and rather verbally aggressive. She tried at first to attend to her wifely duties, but soon husband and wife fell out. She remained frigid and then became pathologically jealous of him, imagining he was having affairs with other women. She would stay mute for weeks on end, and neglected her housework. Then a decisive event occurred – eight months after the marriage her eldest sister came to live with them after the death of her own husband, many years her senior. This sister had had a hysterectomy at the age of 27, for some unknown reason, and was ruled by a great need to mother someone. She took over the household duties, then took over Aimée's husband and tried to rear their child, while criticizing Aimée's conduct and morals. However, she also filled an emotional void in the life of Aimée, who passively accepted her sister's domination.

Lacan was struck by the contrast between the *words* Aimée used to praise her sister's qualities, and her habitually ice-cold *tone*, indicative of extreme but unrecognized ambivalence towards the woman. Only occasionally, when her attention was distracted, was she able to express in words her real feelings of resentment. Here it is also worth mentioning the peculiar attitude Aimée had towards her job: she was devoted to it to such an extent that she was nicknamed the 'workhorse' by her colleagues, though at the same time she professed to despise it. This attitude was an example of what Lacan called a 'vital conflict' in Aimée's personality, although such conflicts were more striking in the case of the ambivalent relationships that she had with the important people in her life (e.g., her sister, son, friend, husband) which were made up of extremes of devotion and contempt.

Aimée's symptoms began to appear at the age of 28, when, after four years of marriage and still working in the same office as her husband, she became pregnant. She began to think that her colleagues were talking against her and criticizing her conduct. She thought that people in the street were whispering about her and despised her, that there were newspaper articles directed against her and threatening to kill her unborn child. She was tormented by nightmares of coffins, she once cut up the tyres of a colleague's bicycle with a knife, and one night threw a pitcher of water and then an iron at her husband. Nevertheless she enthusiastically prepared clothes for the child. But the baby, a girl, was stillborn, choked by the umbilical cord, and from this point the crystallization of Aimée's hostile delusions began. When her friend, who was now living in another town, phoned up after the delivery Aimée considered it strange and felt delusionally convinced that the woman must have been responsible for the baby's death. She stopped attending church, and spent many hours hostile, mute and locked indoors.

The following year, however, Aimée gave birth to a second child – a boy. During her pregnancy she was depressed and her delusions continued, but after the birth she became passionately attached to the boy, refusing to let anyone else look after him for the first five months. She breast-fed him for fourteen months, during which time she became more and more hostile, querulous, and afraid that others might harm him. Meanwhile her sister began to impose her will on Aimée and wanted to be in charge of the child's education. It was now that Aimée's delusions intensified. She applied for a permit to go to America, where she was going to make her fortune as a writer for the sake of her child, whom she had begun to neglect; meanwhile she had delusions that her child had been taken away. Her family had her placed in a mental hospital (all this was some six years before the incident with the actress), and she remained there for six months in an acute psychotic state, with delusions and hallucinations. The family then removed her into their own care, not cured but able to look after the child, although soon after this her sister and her husband took charge of him.

At her own request she was transferred to Paris, where, alone and isolated, her delusions continued to flourish. The actress she later stabbed (not named in the thesis), Sarah Ber-

nhardt, and a successful woman writer became her main persecutors, and she thought that they wanted to harm her
child, whom she managed to visit sporadically. She also
began to write literary pieces for publication. Lacan considered this work very important as clinical material, as it
revealed many aspects of her mental state at the time of the
delusions, as well as highlighting various aspects of her personality and the relations between creativity and the psychotic state. For example, Aimée railed against her women persecutors because they were famous, adulated by the public
and living in luxury, corruption and falseness; while she herself desperately wanted to be a famous writer and to have an
influence on the world. But she was able to convey these
conflicts poetically and, as it were, give to her acute delusional ideas a 'higher level' of expression in her writings.

She claimed to hate artists, poets and journalists, as they
had ganged up to provoke murder, war and corruption
which they then relished. But she herself wanted peace and
brotherly love between all peoples and races. She longed for
the reign of children and women, who would be dressed in
white; the reign of evil on earth would disappear; there
would be no war and all people would be united. She expressed intense love for children and hatred for the cruelty of
adults and for frivolous mothers. The world was heading for
war (not untrue) and she hoped that the English Prince of
Wales would hold a conference at Geneva to bring peace to
troubled Europe. In fact she turned to the Prince many
times, at first for protection against another persecutor, a
well-known writer to whom she had appealed on her first
admission but then accused of some vague liaison with the
actresses. Later on she expressed her platonic love for the
Prince of Wales in her letters, two novels and poetry all of
which she dedicated and sent to him. They were later
returned by Buckingham Palace with a dry note from a private secretary.

Aimée also had a short period of 'dissipation', as she called it later, when she stopped men in the street to tell them her ideas, and invite them to sleep with her; she also felt a 'great curiosity about men's thoughts'.

A few months before the attack on the actress, she assaulted an employee of a publisher who had rejected her writings. She was fined but her mental state was not taken seriously, presumably as it was considered understandable. Just before the attack, she returned to her husband and sister, and did not leave her child's side, as she was in perpetual fear for his life (the child was now aged seven). But eventually he became upset, and she was persuaded to leave him alone. After this, she became increasingly distracted, returned to Paris, bought a knife and reasoned like this: she had to *look* her enemy in the eye. What would the actress think of her if she did not show that she could defend her child? She would think she was a negligent mother. So, she finally went to the theatre, just before she was due to visit her son, and carried out the attack. She was detained in prison where her delusions continued, and she felt alone, miserable and unprotected.

Suddenly, after twenty days, she began to cry and her delusions disappeared – 'The good and the bad' went, she said later. When she was admitted to hospital, she talked lucidly about her life and the delusions, which she mainly considered ridiculous, although she also mentioned that she had acted as she had because people had wanted to kill her son. The boy continued to be the sole object of her concern. She became afraid that she would have to divorce her husband and then lose contact with her child. She wrote a note to Lacan the tone of which was rather ambiguous, as one could not be sure from it how much of her delusional world she had really renounced.

> She [the sister] knows that I am very independent. I was devoted to an *ideal* [our italics], a sort of mission, the love for the human race to which I subordinated everything. I

followed it with ever-increasing perseverance. I went so far as to detach myself from earthly things, and I turned all my suffering to the wrong that desolates the earth. . . Now that events have made my plans more modest I will no longer torment myself for imaginary causes and I will cultivate the calm expansion of my soul. I will be careful that my sister and son do not complain about me, because of my lack of interest (p.177).

In a long and complex discussion Lacan then related the evolution of Aimée's delusions to certain events in her life and to the conflicts in her personality. We will outline some of his main points. The delusions began to crystallize around the person of her ex-friend at the time of the still birth. For this once close friend who had dominated her like her sister before her, Aimée reserved all the hate and resentment she had previously felt towards her sister: her feelings were deflected from one object to another. The delusional system as a whole could thus be seen as involving a deflection of hate from its direct object, which remained *unrecognized* by the subject ('dont elle veut méconnaître l'object direct'), while substitutes far enough away to be safe from attack were charged with all the effective conflicts and pressures. Although Aimée did not hesitate to accuse her once closest friend of hostile intentions, she could not do the same with her sister. She failed to recognize consciously her hate for her, as her sister was in turn the direct substitute for her beloved mother. Moreover, the exalted motherly, platonic love which Aimée expressed in her writings was the other element of her affective conflict with her sister. Mother-love and her resentful feelings were unrecognized at one level and recognized at another. Recognition (reconnaissance) took place at the unconscious level, which Lacan was interested in exploring through Aimée's accounts of her life, her delusional ideas and her writings. Thus when Aimée talked about her sister, it was with words of praise but with an ice-cold tone – the recognition of her hostile attitude remained unconscious.

When Aimée returned to her family from the six-month stay in the mental hospital, she again looked after her son, but after a while obtained permission to be transferred to Paris where she lived alone and in isolation (her 'independence'), allowing her sister to replace her totally as wife and mother. This situation of 'vital conflict' seemed to give fuel to her delusions, which increased in intensity and elaboration. The more she was 'freed' from her responsibilities as a mother and as a family member, and pursued her 'liberation' from them, the more her delusional symptoms constituted themselves. They pushed out of the delusional system at this time in what Lacan called 'thrusts' (poussées), cited by him as an example of the 'fertile moments' (moments féconds) of a delusion.

The delusional system broke down when Aimée moved from the delusional idea to the act – that is, when she wanted to *look* her enemy in the eye and recognize her, which then led to the attack on the actress. Even though the act in itself did not bring any immediate relief, it took Aimée one step away from the stubborn, enveloping delusional system towards a different level of recognition – in this case to an external confrontation where she 'looked the consequences in the eye'.

The existence of several persecutors, and the absence of a real relationship between them and Aimée, emphasized their symbolic meaning in the delusion. They seemed to represent the reproaching sister, and Aimée's image of herself with all its contrasting characteristics, and her unfulfilled ambitions. By hating the persecutors she in effect protected her sister from her hate, and this element of protection was another important function of the delusions. The persecutors tended to follow a type, representing for her the image of a woman who could enjoy freedom and social power, the kind of woman she dreamed of becoming, who represented her *ideal.* Thus the same image which represented her ideal was also the object of her hate.

By means of the stabbing, she turned her persecutor into her victim. What she stabbed in her victim was only the symbol of her own idea. One could see, in the *paranoid structure*, how the images were turned into persecutors or 'internal enemies', and externalized as symbols. At the moment of the gesture itself Aimée's delusions found no immediate relief, but when she was found guilty before the law and imprisoned the delusions disappeared. Presumably this was because when she herself was punished directly by the law, she realized that the target of her attack was herself, and that the actress meant no harm. It was as if the paranoid structure had accomplished another of its purposes – the carrying out of self-punishment by the law – and that the wish behind the delusions was one of unconscious self-punishment, probably in order to deal with her enormous guilt over her attitude to her child because of her desire to live a free and liberated life. For this reason, Lacan suggested that Aimée's psychosis merited a separate clinical category with a good prognosis – 'self-punishment paranoia' (paranoia d'autopunition), a term which owed its origin to Freud's concept (SE 14, pp. 332-333) of those who are 'criminals from a sense of guilt'. Freud described how certain criminal acts give relief to subjects who suffer from oppressive feelings of guilt before the crime. He also described how children can be quite often naughty on purpose to provoke punishment, and then are quiet and happy after the punishment.

Aimée's life was dominated by gross, unrecognized conflicts within her personality. The delusional system attempted to deal with these conflicts by turning them into external persecutors. This was a way of keeping the conflicts at a distance from herself, but, of course, they were still her internal enemies as they arose from within herself and continued to harass her. She was dominated by her delusions as she was dominated by her real objects. It was only when she finally took an active role, in the attack, even though against a displaced target, that she came closer to recognizing that her real target was herself. Lacan linked in detail these conflicts in her personality to psychoanalytic concepts of psychical structure and personality development. In brief, he considered that there was a fixation, or disturbance, at an early stage of super-ego formation, the stage when the subject is assimilating the constraints and ideals of his parents and their substitutes, and is becoming a social being. We will return to this topic briefly in the next chapter (see p. 51) when we discuss some of Freud's concepts.

One of the important themes of the thesis was the role of Aimée's ideal images, which became targets for her conflicting love and hate. Perhaps one could trace a connection between Lacan's interest in the role of ideal images and his formulation of the mirror phase four years later, where he was to elaborate the role of the image in the subject's personality.

The thesis was a generally successful attempt to make psychological sense of paranoid psychosis, in which Lacan tried to uncover the psychological structures underlying the psychosis, by examining the relations between the psychosis and the patient's biography, intentions and motives. He considered that he had demonstrated the importance of the role of méconnaissance, the refusal to recognize wishes and desires, in psychosis. Méconnaissance reveals itself when the psychotic patient wants to impose his own intentions on what he perceives as, for example, the chaos of the world. The patient does not perceive that this world chaos is really a manifestation of his own chaotic being, and that what he takes to be his true intentions are really only the 'reverse image' of his own being. Thus Aimée railed against negligent mothers, but was a negligent mother herself. Freud described a similar phenomenon in his descriptions of 'projection' (SE 12, p.63), the mechanism whereby the subject refuses to recognize certain wishes as his own, and attributes them instead to other people.

44

Along with the description of méconnaissance, which emphasized Aimée's failure to recognize knowledge about herself, Lacan also showed that there is what one could call 'paranoid knowledge': knowledge that belongs to the paranoid structure, and makes sense if one undertakes a detailed history. Thus Aimée's fear of being a negligent mother was transformed, in the paranoid structure, into a hate of negligent mothers – knowledge of her fear was produced in a paranoid form, which can be interpreted by the physician. Paranoid knowledge is based on the sense of persecution, and has a generalized irrational element, e.g., the fear of being attacked by anonymous persecutors; but it also contains elements of the subject's personality, and so an exploration of such forms of knowledge can provide insights into the subject's psyche. Lacan considered that paranoid knowledge is not only a clinical fact, but corresponds to the stage in the subject's genesis when ego and objects are first being distinguished, and when in addition both ego and objects are becoming imbued with aspects of permanence, identity and substantiality.

Lacan appears to infer that the very structure of the ego, on which personality is based, is paranoid. One can indeed see in the structure of paranoid knowledge some equivalence to the childhood phenomenon of what Lacan called 'transitivism' – the child who strikes another says he has been struck, and the child who sees another fall, cries (see below, p. 58). One can also see how this concept leads on to that of the mirror stage, in which Lacan described the formation of the ego in more detail, and within a clearly psychoanalytic framework. (In parenthesis, it is interesting to note that paranoia was a concern of the surrealists as well. For example, Salvador Dali in 1930 wrote in 'La femme invisible' (quoted in Rosemont, 1978 p. 137), that he used the 'paranoid-critical method' in his art. This was a 'spontaneous method of "irrational knowledge" based on the critical and systematic objectification of delirious associations and interpretations'.)

The topic of psychosis remained important for Lacan in his later work. He was fascinated by the psychotic's means of communication, the strange allusions and associations, verbal games, neologisms, and the various ways in psychosis that language can be fragmented. In the psychotic patient one seems to detect the limits of language, yet Lacan was at pains to emphasize that madness has a meaning. There is an almost 'anti-psychiatry' attitude in the thesis which is similar to that of Laing, the radical psychiatrist and author of *The Divided Self*. Both Laing and Lacan emphasized that madness has a meaningful structure, and both were dissatisfied with the traditional, orthodox psychiatric model, although in Lacan's case there is less social polemic. The thesis also displays a refusal to be confined within the usual professional limits in that it includes references to and discussion of many thinkers such as Spinoza, Bergson, Descartes, James and Russell. The thesis not only contained several of the themes that would occupy Lacan in later years, but also marked the beginning of his style.

CHAPTER TWO

'THE MIRROR STAGE'
(1936)

BY 1934, Lacan had joined the Société Psychanalytique
de Paris, of which he became a full member just
before the war. In 1936 he presented his paper on the
mirror stage to the International Psychoanalytic Congress in
Marienbad, but it was not published. Its contents are outlined in his article on the family in the Encyclopédie Française (1938), while the paper in the *Ecrits* (1966) is a revised
version which he delivered at the Zurich International
Psychoanalytic Congress in 1949.

The mirror stage was a new addition to psychoanalytic
theory, and we will give a short account of some of the relevant classical psychoanalytic concepts before tackling Lacan's
contribution. These proposed some revision of the concepts
of the ego and of narcissism.

In Freud's theory of the mind, the psychical apparatus was
differentiated into a number of systems or 'agencies', each of
which had distinct properties and functions, but which
interacted dynamically and in conflict with each other.*
Two theories of these agencies can be identified in Freud's
writings. The first theory, dating from about 1900 – the 'first
topography' – distinguishes between the unconscious, preconscious and conscious, while the 'second topography',

---

* In chapter 6 (p. 107) we argue that the old English word 'instance'
is more faithful to Freud's use of the German 'Instanz' than
'agency'.

dating from 1923, differentiates the three agencies of id, ego and super-ego (Das Es, Das Ich, Das Über-Ich). There is overlap between these two models, e.g., the ego and super-ego are partly preconscious and partly unconscious.

In the first topography the situation is as follows:

The unconscious consists of wishful impulses ('drive representatives') which seek to discharge. They exist side by side without being influenced by each other, and are exempt from mutual contradiction. Unconscious processes are subject to the seeking of pleasure and avoidance of pain, to the so-called 'pleasure principle'. They are also governed by the primary process, which means that there is a great mobility in the psychical energy attached to unconscious ideas – a mobility of 'cathexis', the word traditionally used to translate Freud's term 'Besetzung', literally in German 'occupation'. Thus one idea may surrender to another idea all its quota of cathexis by the process of 'displacement', or appropriate the cathexis of several other ideas by the process of 'condensation'.

The preconscious is quite distinct from the unconscious. Preconscious contents differ from those of the unconscious in that they are in principle accessible to consciousness, e.g., as memories that are available to consciousness but not actually yet conscious. The preconscious and the conscious are governed by the secondary process, which coincides with waking thought, judgement, reasoning and controlled action. In the primary process psychical energy flows freely, while in the secondary process energy is much more bound and flows in a more controlled way. Satisfaction is postponed, allowing for an assessment of external circumstances. This corresponds to the 'reality principle', a concept discussed by Lacan with a new emphasis in his paper 'Beyond the reality principle' (1936), which we will describe in the next chapter.

The conscious is closely linked to the organs of perception. Consciousness is a function of the perception-conscious system, which receives information made up of sensations from internal and external sources. In *The Interpretation of Dreams*, Freud viewed the conscious as a 'sense-organ for the perception of psychical qualities' (SE5, p. 615). Although consciousness provides us with a sketchy picture of our mental processes, it is of great importance whether or not a psychical phenomenon can be recognized consciously. Painful or forbidden thoughts can be refused entry into the conscious by repression, but remain dynamically active in the unconscious, where they are seeking expression. They seek re-entry into the conscious, but can only gain access indirectly, e.g., symbolically in symptoms, in dreams, or in slips of the tongue and jokes, and they are then called 'derivatives of the unconscious'.

The ego in the first topography has various roles. In Freud's pre-analytic 'Project for a Scientific Psychology' (1895), its prime function is that of inhibition. Its neurological basis is that of an organization of nerve-cells with relatively stable boundaries, and it acts as a store of energy which enables it to send out nerve impulses which can control and attract discharges from other nerve-cells. It particularly acts to inhibit the primary processes we described above, and so to inhibit impulses which might evoke unpleasure. It helps the organism to take account of the external world, and is linked with the secondary processes.

In Freud's early psychoanalytic papers, the ego is a defensive agency which fends off unacceptable ideas from consciousness. With the introduction of his first topography, however, the role of the ego becomes less clear. It still appears to function in mechanisms of defence, for example, in the 'Rat Man' case (1909), it is the agency which opposes itself to unconscious wishes. Then with the introduction of the concept of narcissism, 1909-1914, based on observations on homosexual and psychotic patients, the ego is conceived in a new way. A unified ego is not present from birth but has to be developed. There are, though, auto-erotic drives

49

which take place without any overall organization. The infant obtains satisfaction from his own body without the need of an external object, e.g., in thumb-sucking. For the ego to be formed, a 'new psychical action' (eine neue psychische Aktion) has to take place in order to bring about the stage of narcissism (SE 14, p. 77). The stage of narcissism occurs between auto-eroticism and the relationship with an external human object, when the individual's own body is taken as his love-object.

> There comes a time in the development of the individual at which he unifies his sexual drives (which have hitherto been engaged in auto-erotic activities) in order to obtain a love-object; and he begins by taking his own body as his love-object, and only subsequently proceeds from this to the choice of some person other than himself (SE 12, pp. 60-61).

Presumably, the ego in this scheme is formed at the stage of narcissism, between the stages of auto-eroticism and object love, while being itself taken as a love-object. But it is not clear in Freud what is this new psychical action that brings about ego formation, though we are told that the ego first picks out objects by identification and by incorporating objects into itself. Here one is dealing with fundamental dilemmas in analytic theory, and Lacan's mirror stage offers a new formulation of the problem of ego formation.

The second topography clarified a number of Freud's ideas. Once again the three agencies are in a dynamic relationship. The id has all the characteristics of the unconscious and it is the store of drives. Then under the influence of the external world, one portion of the id undergoes a special development. 'From what was originally a cortical layer, equipped with the organs for receiving stimuli, and with the arrangements for acting as a protective shield, a special organization has arisen which henceforward acts as an intermediary between the id and the external world . . . the ego' (SE 23, p. 145).

The ego is not only formed under the influence of the external world, but also by contributions from the person's own body, particularly the surface. 'The ego is ultimately derived from bodily sensations, chiefly from those springing from the surface of the body. It may thus be regarded as a mental projection of the surface of the body, besides representing the superficies of the mental apparatus' (SE 19, p. 26). The ego's functions include voluntary movement control, memory, flight, adaptation and learning. It also strives to avoid unpleasure. Any increase in unpleasure is met by a signal of anxiety, which sets off its defensive actions.

On the surface of the ego lies the consciousness-perception system, while the inside of the ego is partly made up of preconscious processes, particularly linked with speech; but a large part of it is unconscious. It should be said that Freud emphasized that these descriptions of locality were metaphors for the complex workings of the mental apparatus.

The super-ego is like the conscience and is formed by the internalization, through a complicated process of identification, of parental demands, prohibitions and ideal images (which in Aimée's case were turned into internal enemies). 'The long period of childhood, during which the growing human being lives in dependence on his parents, leaves behind it as a precipitate the formation in the ego of a special agency in which this parental influence is prolonged . . . the super-ego' (SE 23, p. 146). The super-ego, in fact, comprises both a critical, self-observing and punishing function, and also the setting up of ideal goals derived from the 'ego-ideal'. The notion of the ego-ideal, which preceded the second topography, brings into a basically persecuting and aggressive super-ego (with which it is difficult to identify) a narcissistic element, the love for one's own ideal. What the individual projects before him as his ideal is the substitute for the lost narcissism of his childhood in which he was his own ideal. We have already seen in Aimée's case how her ideal images and the beliefs of her delusions were charged both with extreme resentment and love, and how difficult it was for her to bring together these conflicting feelings.

In his formulation of the mirror stage Lacan used Freud's concept of narcissism, and some of his formulations on ego formation. In trying to identify the 'new psychical action' that was meant to bring about ego formation, Lacan seems to agree with the idea that the ego is not present from birth, and instead has to be developed; but he disagreed with certain aspects of Freud's formulation of the ego in the second topography. In particular, he thought there was not enough emphasis on the ego's function of méconnaissance – the refusal to acknowledge thoughts and feelings – and that the later Freud put too much emphasis on the ego's adaptive functions. We will return to this point after we have described the mirror stage.

The mirror stage was viewed by Lacan as a formative event in the development of the subject, occurs roughly between the age of six and eighteen months when the infant begins to recognize his image in the mirror. This event has been observed with babies looking at themselves in the mirror, and is also based on studies of animal behaviour made by psychologists as well as on psychoanalytic work.

The recognition may be accompanied by pleasure. The child is fascinated by the image and seems to be trying to control and play with it, so that one may observe that,

> unable as yet to walk, or even to stand up, and held tightly as he is by some support, human or artificial . . . he nevertheless overcomes in a flutter of jubilant activity, the obstruction of his support and, fixing his attitude in a slightly leaning-forward position, in order to hold it in his gaze, brings back an instantaneous aspect of the image (E, pp. 1-2).

One can observe the 'signs of triumphant jubilation and

playful discovery that characterize, from the sixth month, the child's encounter with his image in the mirror' (E, p. 18). To illustrate Lacan's point, we have found useful the work of Wolfgang Köhler with chimpanzees. Chimpanzees are also fascinated by their mirror image, and in ways that shed light on human activity. Thus Köhler wrote that

> Rana [a chimpanzee] . . . gazed long and intently into the mirror, looked up and then down, put it to her face and licked it once, started into it again, and suddenly her free hand rose and grasped – as though at a body behind the mirror. But as she grasped emptiness she dropped the mirror sideways in her astonishment. Then she lifted it again, stared fixedly at the other ape, and again was misled into grasping into empty space. She became impatient and struck out violently behind the mirror. . . She held the mirror still in one hand, drew back the other arm as far as possible behind her back, gazed with an air of indifference at the other animal, then suddenly made a pounce with her free hand. However, both she and the rest soon became used to this side of the affair, and concentrated all their interest on the image; this interest did not decrease . . . but remained so strong that the playing with reflecting surfaces became one of the most popular and permanent of their "fashions" (Köhler, pp. 268-9).

As with the chimpanzee, the human infant seems to go through an initial stage of confusing the image with reality, and may try to grasp hold of the image behind the mirror, or seize hold of the supporting adult. Then comes the discovery of the existence of an image with its own properties. Finally, there is the realization that the image is his own – when he moves his image moves, and so on. It might be that the chimpanzee does not recognize what he sees as his own image, unlike the child, and that this is what distinguishes the human as a subject from the animal who merely remains fascinated by reflections.

Babies are from birth intensely interested in what is going on around them, and respond to many aspects of their parents' activity, but the mirror stage is a particular moment when the infant's response is of a different order. Of course, an infant may never actually see a real mirror reflecting himself. In this case he may not have an image of himself which is distinct from the mother's gaze. Lacan's mirror stage refers to a particular moment of recognition and jubilation, when the infant is moving away from the simple reflection of the mother's gaze.

Lacan begins his account with the first months of the infant's life. The infant from birth does not have overall sensorimotor co-ordination, and the main motor pathways leading to his limbs do not mature (myelinate) until the second year (Freud called this 'motor helplessness'). He is also very dependent on external care. So he is relatively unco-ordinated, helpless and dependent, and these first months of life are full of anxiety, uneasiness and 'discord'. Lacan referred in this context to a biological factor – man's 'specific prematurity of birth'. The infant's body is relatively immature and takes a long time to develop, and he is dependent on others for longer than any other animal. There is a basic deficit, a lack of co-ordination and fragmentation of functions.

At a certain point, around six months, and presumably when the perceptual apparatus has reached a certain stage of development, the infant becomes aware, through seeing his image in the mirror, of his own body as a totality, a total form or *Gestalt*. The mirror image is held together, it can come and go with a slight change of the infant's position, and his mastery of the image fills him with triumph and joy. The mirror image anticipates the mastery of his body that the infant has not yet objectively achieved. He falls in love with his image and, in contrast to the auto-erotic stage, in which he has an erotic relationship to his fragmented body, he now takes the image of his whole body as his love-object. Lacan's description here is very close to Freud's of the narcissistic stage, when the body is taken as love-object. Thus the infant's *imaginary* mastery of his body anticipates his biological mastery. In Lacan's view, any future relation with reality will be marked by this imaginary anticipation. 'The mirror stage is a drama whose internal thrust is precipitated from insufficiency to anticipation' (E, p. 4). There is then a fundamental 'alienation' in this action. The infant's mastery is in the mirror image, outside himself, while he is not really master of his movements. He only sees his form as more or less total and unified in an external image, in a virtual, alienated, ideal unity that cannot actually be touched. Alienation is this lack of being by which his realization lies in another actual or imaginary space.

This image of unity is not disturbed by the turbulent movements of the infant's unco-ordinated body. It is a mirage in a *Gestalt*, that is, an external form, which the mirror reflects back in a reversed symmetry and perspective. The infant's movements and bodily prematurity are reversed in the fixity of a big 'statue' of himself. 'This *Gestalt* . . . in these two aspects of its appearing [of fixity and stature] symbolizes the ego's mental permanence and at the same time prefigures its alienating fate, the statue into which man projects himself' (E, pp. 2-3).

In Lacan's view the formation of the ego commences at the point of alienation and fascination with one's own image. This image is the first organized form in which the individual identifies himself, so the ego takes its form from, and is formed by, the organizing and constitutive qualities of this image. The mirror image organizes and constitutes the subject's vision of the world, and Lacan cited examples from biology to demonstrate the organizing function of the image. 'It is a necessary condition for the maturation of the gonad of the female pigeon,' for example, 'that it should see another member of its species of either sex; so sufficient in itself is this condition that the desired effect may be obtained merely by placing the individual within reach of the field of reflection of a mirror' (E, p. 3).

Nevertheless, as far as the ego's formation is concerned, one can see certain parallels with Freud's thought. We have explained how in Freud's early work, the ego was an organization of nerve cells with relatively stable boundaries, which acted as a store of energy, and this seems similar to a *Gestalt*. In Freud's later work the ego was regarded, in part, as a 'mental projection of the surface of the body'. This is compatible with the notion of a mirror image as a projection of the surface of the body. Finally, Freud's 'new psychical action' that brings about the stage of narcissism seems to be similar to the formative action of the image for the ego at the mirror stage.

The ego for Lacan is thus formed on the basis of an *imaginary* relationship of the subject with his own body. The ego has the illusion of autonomy, but it is only an illusion, and the subject moves from fragmentation and insufficiency to illusory unity. The analyst is familiar with the various images that symbolize fragmentation of the body and ego formation, e.g., in dreams. As Lacan wrote,

The fragmented body manifests itself regularly in dreams when the movement of the analysis encounters a certain level of aggressive disintegration in the individual. It then appears in the form of disjointed limbs, or of those organs, represented in exoscopy, growing wings and taking up arms for intestinal persecutions – the very same that the visionary Hieronymous Bosch has fixed for all time in painting . . . the formation of the ego is symbolized in dreams by a fortress, or a stadium – its inner area and enclosure, surrounded by marshes and rubbish-tips, dividing it into two opposite fields of contest where the subject flounders in quest of the lofty, remote inner castle whose form symbolizes the id in a quite startling way (E, p. 5).

As the dream images show us, the infant experiences this discord between the fragmented self and his unitary image as an aggressive disintegration of his own body. This identification with his own body as 'other' than himself structures the subject as a rival with himself. So although the infant identifies with the visual *Gestalt* of his own body, the body is invested with all the distress and fragmentation from earlier months. Thus in Lacan's view, aggressivity is first of all linked to the images of the fragmented body.

> These are the images of castration, mutilation, dismemberment, dislocation, evisceration, devouring, bursting open of the body. . . One only has to listen to children aged between two and five playing, alone or together, to know that the pulling off of the head and the ripping open of the belly are themes that occur spontaneously to their imagination, and that this is corroborated by the experience of the doll torn to pieces . . . the works of Bosch are an atlas of all the aggressive images that torment mankind . . . [this kind of image] crops up constantly in dreams, especially at the point when analysis appears to be turning its attention on the most fundamental, most archaic fixations. I remember the dream of one of my patients, whose aggressive drives took the form of obsessive phantasies; in the dream he saw himself driving a car, accompanied by the woman with whom he was having a rather difficult affair, pursued by a flying fish, whose skin was so transparent that one could see the horizontal liquid level through the body, an image of vesicle persecution of great anatomical clarity (E, p. 12).

The mirror image inaugurates a new visual and mental experience in the infant's life, since an organized form of himself is seen projected outside, together with the space surrounding him, in the mirror's surface. The infant can then see his image only in relation to the space in which this image is projected, the *Gestalt* establishing a relationship

57

between the organism and the world around it. But this relationship is discordant because it is based on an imaginary and alienating experience. This discordance also determines the discordant nature of the relations with others who occupy the space around the subject's mirror image.

The illusion of autonomy from which the ego takes its origin is limited and contradicted by another important aspect of the *Gestalt*, that is, the fact that it includes in its capturing form the relation between one's image and the circumscribing space. In other words, the mirror stage inaugurates a *spatial identification* and the subsequent conflict with the reflected image of the world. The same conflict which was determined by the fracture between the subject's undifferentiated and fragmented way of being, and the imaginary autonomy with which the subject has identified himself as ego, is continued as the subject identifies with the image of the human form, that is, with other human beings.

Thus even though the infant is his own rival before being a rival of another, he is captured from very early on by the human form and conditioned by the other's look, for example by the face and the gaze of the mother. The mirror stage inaugurates an identification with other human images and with the world the subject shares with them. The primary conflict between identification with, and primordial rivalry with, the other's image, begins a dialectical process that links the ego to more complex social situations.

During this period [the mirror stage] one will record the emotional reactions and the articulated evidences of a normal transitivism. The child who strikes another says that he has been struck; the child who sees another fall, cries. Similarly, it is by means of an identification with the other that he sees the whole gamut of . . . display ['parade'], whose structural ambivalence is clearly revealed in his behaviour, the slave being identified with the despot, the actor with the spectator, the seduced with the seducer (E, p. 19).

In this context Lacan quoted a non-psychoanalytic source. He mentioned a passage from St Augustine's *Confessions*: 'I have myself seen jealousy in an infant and know what it means. He was not old enough to speak, but whenever he saw his foster-brother at the breast, he would grow pale with an envious stare'. Lacan interpreted the observation as one that involved the infant (who could not speak) in a confrontation with his counterpart, as if in front of a mirror. The infant observed, had an emotional reaction (he went pale), and then images of 'primordial frustration' were re-activated (he stared enviously). Lacan described these features of behaviour as the 'psychical and somatic coordinates of original aggressivity' (E, p. 20), and he went on to describe how aggressivity and narcissism appear, from observation, to be tightly bound to one another. They enter into action in every process of identification, whether it be with an image of oneself, with another person, or with fragments of oneself or another.

Analysts disagree on the exact nature of aggressivity, at the point in a baby's development at which one can observe it, and how it is linked to other drives. Melanie Klein, for example, insisted on the prominent role played by the aggressive drives from the earliest stages of infancy. Other analysts consider that it only makes sense to talk of aggressivity when the infant's ego is more organized than it is at birth, and can thus make a more obviously aggressive attack on other objects. Like Klein, Lacan seemed to consider that the roots of a primordial aggressivity could be seen in the earliest months of life, but unlike her he was more concerned with aggressivity as it arises in relation to the mirror stage (for example as it appears in St Augustine's observation), when the infant is arising as a subject in his own right. Aggressivity, for him, is a 'correlative tension of the narcissistic structure in the coming-into-being of the subject' (E, p. 22). Aggressivity is the irreducible accompaniment of narcissism, and is released in any relation with the other, 'even in a relation involving the most Samaritan of aid' (E, p. 6).

Lacan parted company with other analytic schools in his view of the ego. For him, the ego's function is purely imaginary, and through its function the subject tends to become alienated. The ego 'neglects, scotomizes, misconstrues' (E, p. 22); it is an agency organized to misread the truth which comes to the subject from the unconscious; its basic function is that of méconnaissance, the refusal to accept the truth. In fact this view of the ego is nearer to the ego of Freud's first than of his second topography. In the former the ego's defensive properties are emphasized as well as its intimate connection with the stage of narcissism, while in the latter the ego is more clearly connected with the consciousness-perception system.

In Lacan's opinion, the ego cannot in any way be centred on the consciousness-perception system, nor can it be organized by the 'reality principle', with its emphasis on adjustment to external circumstances. This implies that he was absolutely and fundamentally opposed to any idea that one should help the analysand to strengthen his ego, or to help him adjust to society in any way, or that one should help him tolerate unconscious impulses by building up his ego. He was opposed to any notion that psychoanalysis is concerned with producing healthy, well-adjusted individuals who would be able to know what reality is, and who would be in possession of a healthy, tolerant ego. In addition, he considered that the individual was in permanent conflict with his surroundings, and that any notion of a unified, healthy individual who was happy with his adjustment to his surroundings was a méconnaissance of Freud's basic teachings.

This is an extreme and controversial interpretation of Freud. If it is taken literally, it seems to rule out any notion of an analysis of the analysand's defences. The ego for Freud is a defensive agency, warding off impulses from consciousness, and in this sense its prime function is to ignore the unconscious impulses which seek to gain expression in consciousness, and it is an agency designed to ward off unpalatable truths. In classical analysis the ego's defences have a protective role, and we cannot ignore them. In this viewpoint one cannot just plunge into an analysis without a careful consideration of the nature of these defences. Most analysts agree that the ego must acquire an increased tolerance for 'crude' unconscious impulses, so that it can express them more easily both in direct and indirect form, thus increasing the number of choices and satisfactions that can become available to the analysand. They consider that an alteration in the ego can enlarge the analysand's capacity for self-scrutiny and capacity to bear unconscious impulses. Thus at first sight it would seem to be foolhardy to ignore the ego's defensive properties and only concentrate on its alienating properties.

However, there is some evidence that Lacan was aware of the importance of defences when it came to purely therapeutic questions. In the Rome Discourse, for instance, he discussed the necessity of understanding the role of the type of language determined by the ego. Nonetheless, he was still opposed to any idea of adjustment to the social environment, and his writings abound with a tireless polemic against such a notion. In some ways, such an attitude is very refreshing. It puts the emphasis on the workings of the unconscious, and the role of unconscious impulses; and it emphasizes the doubtfulness of the supposed reality with which the ego is trying to deal, by means of information derived from the consciousness-perception system. In Lacan's view, the ego's mastery of the environment is always an illusory mastery, as a result of the way it is formed at the mirror stage, and the human subject will continue throughout life to look for an imaginary 'wholeness' and 'unity'. He will want to master his environment, and feel a unified and total person. It is these quests, which for Lacan are futile, which are controlled by the ego.

Lacan considered that the mistake of many analysts, including the later Freud, was to confuse the human subject with the ego. The notion of the 'subject' is indeed more philosophical than psychoanalytic, and Freud himself rarely mentioned the concept of a subject; he usually referred to the 'individual', or to the individual's 'psychical apparatus', which was differentiated into the various agencies. He occasionally mentioned a 'self', but it was often confused with the ego, at least in the days of his first topography. On the other hand, he quite often referred to the 'eigene Person' (the person as an individual), and it is perhaps in this sense that one can talk of the 'subject'. This subject seems to have a psychical apparatus made up of various agencies, each of which has distinct properties and functions, and which interact dynamically and in conflict with each other; but it is not at all clear whether for Freud there is an additional concept of a unifying total 'self', which draws together all these agencies. Lacan considered that this cannot be found in Freud, and himself thought that the subject could only be grasped as a series of rather unstable tensions, and remains somewhat elusive. The ego might give a feeling of permanence and stability to the subject, but this is an illusion.

Lacan considered that the psychoanalytic relationship was one between subjects, and so could not be reduced to a relationship between two unified, stable individuals, with easily objectifiable psychological properties. It is not easy to grasp this notion, except perhaps within an analytic relationship, where thoughts and feelings often seem to come and go in a fluid and contradictory manner. In this context, Lacan's concept of the elusive subject seems to make sense, at the very least as a description of what takes place in the analytic relationship. But he certainly did not consider that the subject was totally elusive. In his view, it was through language that the subject could be grasped. In the next chapter, we describe Lacan's early attempts to outline a comprehensive theory of the subject, through considering the role of language.

CHAPTER THREE

'BEYOND
THE REALITY PRINCIPLE'
(1936)

I N HIS THESIS Lacan had criticized the concept of
psychosis determined by an organic process based on
the scientific model, and opposed to it the notion of
human meaning and psychogenesis. In the *Ecrits* (1966), in a
short account of his position at that time – 'My previous history' ('De nos antécédents', e, pp. 65-72) – he wrote that he
was soon led on to considering the question of the relation
between science and psychoanalysis, and in particular
whether or not psychoanalysis could claim its own realm of
knowledge independent of the positive sciences (such as
physics, chemistry and biology, which use traditional scientific methodology). In 'Beyond the Reality Principle' Lacan
discussed the possibility of studying human phenomena
with a different methodology from that of the traditional
sciences, such as that used by the human sciences, but using
the insights of psychoanalysis.

The paper covers a wide range of issues, and includes one
of Lacan's first accounts of the role of language in
psychoanalysis. He attacked traditional psychology based
on the positive sciences, and opposed to it the notion of
human meaning produced by means of language, as he had
done in the thesis, though with more emphasis. That is, he
was searching for a 'non-positivist' framework for
psychoanalysis.

According to Lacan, psychoanalysis has not given
enough consideration to the fact that Freud's psychoanalytic

discoveries were based on the science of his time, but moved away from the scientific viewpoint and became related to other disciplines such as philosophy, anthropology, art and literature. While Freud was making his discoveries, he often had to give them some scientific justification, although he also turned to other disciplines as a source of knowledge. Lacan felt that there was a need to redefine the status of psychoanalytic knowledge in the light of a new cultural context. For example, he thought that Freud could not have avoided a fruitful confrontation with linguistics or structural anthropology, or what are now called the 'human sciences', those disciplines essentially concerned with human meaning and the nature of the subject.

Lacan considered that a major task for psychoanalysis is to make its own knowledge legitimate by identifying as much as it can its own method and field of investigation, while continuing to open up a dialogue with contemporary natural and human sciences. Epistemology being the theory of knowledge, this was what he meant when he proposed an epistemological discourse to the analyst, the 'one who is supposed to know' what he does when he practises psychoanalysis. Lacan based this discourse on a questioning of Freud's reality principle, on which most post-Freudian analysts have based their interventions. He raised the problem of the *object of psychology*, and the dilemma of whether or not psychology could be made into a science. That is, he asked of what kind of knowledge psychology made itself the 'guarantor', and what was its autonomy with respect to other sciences. This was at the time a novel approach to the problems of psychoanalysis; and although the nature of psychology has considerably changed since the mid-thirties, the paper does raise important issues; whatever one's standpoint in relation to science, Lacan does make an attempt to discuss the relevant issues in a rigorous fashion.

From this essay onwards, Lacan attempted to situate psychoanalysis predominantly within language. Many analysts would probably now agree that psychoanalysis can- not be conceived as a natural science of human behaviour like behavioural psychology or orthodox psychiatry. But there are not many analysts who would go along with Lacan's extreme ideas about language and psychoanalysis, even if they would agree that psychoanalysis is essentially concerned with the nature of human meaning.

The main body of the essay begins with an enigmatic phrase set out in capital letters, which we have translated as follows: 'ALTHOUGH LIMITED TO FACTS ABOUT DESIRE, PSYCHOLOGY BECAME A SCIENCE AFTER FREUD HAD ESTABLISHED THE RELATIV- ITY OF ITS OBJECT.' As can be seen, Lacan's obscure style was already in evidence in the mid-thirties. Indeed, it remained a typical feature of his essays to begin with an epig- ram, which would have some explicit connection with the text, or contain or anticipate metaphorically the core of the essay's issues.

Following the epigram, there are criticisms of various contemporary approaches to psychology, approaches which have little relevance nowadays. Then Lacan outlines his attempt to look for the basis of which a science of psychology could be constituted. It was his opinion that the Freudian revolution subverted the traditional basis of psychology, although the later Freud and the second gener- ation of psychoanalysts had tried to escape from this subver- sion. The following is the basis of his argument:

Freud's reality principle was described in detail in the essay 'Formulations on the two principles of mental func- tioning' (1911), and in the book *Beyond the Pleasure Princi- ple* (1920). We have already pointed out how Freud intro- duced a 'new psychical action' between auto-eroticism and object love, a new mediating action between the original id and the external world. In Freud's view, the external world interfered with the pursuit of pleasure, the principle govern- ing the primary mental processes. The ego appeared as the

representation of the surface of the body as well as the superficies of the mental apparatus, as the shield which protects
the pleasure-seeking drives in the id from the interfering
stimuli of the external world. Freud proposed that the ego
arises with the setting up of the reality principle, which,
though independent of the pleasure principle, does not
develop in opposition to it. The ego neutralizes the demands
of the world outside mental reality. For Freud, the reality
principle is still at the service of pleasure, but it imposes
deviations and delays to achieve it.

Lacan then added his concept of the mirror stage to the
argument about the reality principle. Any recognition,
acceptance or rejection of the world through the agency of
the ego has its origin in the frozen and precarious unity of
the image of the body appearing outside as a *Gestalt* in the
world. In Lacan's view, the world starts to exist for man
only in the projection of himself into that world. Thus a
sense of reality depends on human, or psychical, reality.
Hence the proper field of a psychology, which is open to scientific investigation, is that of psychical reality. This is in
fact compatible with Freud's earlier views on the nature of
the ego.

The idea of psychical reality (psychische Realität) arose
early in the history of psychoanalysis, when Freud realized
that his patients' ideas of being seduced were mainly phantasies. In the second topography, however Freud
emphasized rather the adaptive functions of the ego, which
was then concerned to adapt the individual to external
realities. The American ego psychologists took up this
notion in considerable detail. Melanie Klein, on the other
hand, put more emphasis on the importance of psychical
reality, and in particular on the persistence of infantile
anxieties in the mature adult. Lacan took the view that he
both deplored any idea of the ego as an adaptive agency,
indeed any idea of adaptation in general, and also tended to
play down the importance of infantile anxieties in the adult.

Lacan considered that the human subject is fundamentally in conflict with the environment, both in relation to the world of physical nature, and to the social world with all its laws and rules which affect the relation of subjects to each other. For him, this also meant that one had to take into account the subject's problematic relationship to his own truth.

In this essay Lacan's concept of truth seems to be related to the nature of psychic reality or what is *true for the subject*. He considered that Freud's new work involved a novel formulation of the method of study, and the status of the object, of psychology. Freud's basic assumption, according to Lacan, is that in general truth is 'relative' to the object of study, and that in particular the analytic object of study is 'relative' to a study of the facts of desire. This rather obscure concept of 'relativity' seems to mean that the facts of desire are as real to the subject as the facts of nature viewed by positive science. Thus when traditional psychology contrasted psychical phenomena such as beliefs, delusions, intuitions and dreams, with the operations of rational knowledge considered as the proper guarantor of truth, it classified phenomena on the basis of *values*, giving priority to some phenomena over others. For example, the image was considered as only an illusion of the senses, and it was reduced to the rank of a shadow. In this scheme, beliefs, dreams, and images are not recognized as real, but belong to a delusional reality, as they do not fit in with the mechanistic viewpoint of natural science. The role of traditional psychology was then to subordinate these phenomena to a hierarchical system of values. Freud, instead, showed that these apparently trivial phenomena had meaning, and that they were of vital importance in understanding the human subject. By limiting itself in its attitude to these phenomena, traditional psychology had deprived itself of its unique object and means of study.

Of course, psychology has come a long way since the 1930s, and there are many branches of the discipline that are concerned with human phenomena within a non-positivist framework – no doubt thanks in part to the Freudian revolution. When he wrote the paper Lacan felt that because of psychology's failure, there needed to be a psychoanalytic reflection on positivism itself, and a re-examination of the foundations of traditional science. As he wrote,

> Do not misunderstand me. I am not playing with the paradox of denying that science has no knowledge of truth. But I do not forget that truth is a value which responds to man's uncertainty about himself, marked phenomenologically by his lived experience, and that the search for truth has historically motivated the goals of the mystic and the rules of the moralist, the paths of the ascetic and the findings of the mystagogue, under the heading of the spiritual. This research, which has imposed on the whole of culture the pre-eminence of the evidence of truth, has created a moral attitude which has been and still is for science a condition of its existence. But truth in its specific value remains a stranger to the scientific order: science can honour itself by an alliance with truth; . . . but it cannot by any means identify it as its own end (e, p. 79).

In his attempt to define a new way of studying human phenomena Lacan was deeply influenced by the methods of phenomenology. The latter literally means the study or description of appearances. A phenomenology may refer to any sustained and penetrating description of how things appear. However, the term may be used specifically to refer to the method of enquiry elaborated by the German philosopher Edmund Husserl (1859-1938). He took philosophy to begin from an exact inspection of mental processes in which all assumptions about the causation of these processes are bracketed. He considered that phenomenology was not an empirical technique, but a logical investigation of essences or meanings. Recent philosophers who have developed their own versions of phenomenology include Jean-Paul Sartre, whose existentialism Lacan criticized, and Maurice Merleau-Ponty whose work affected his greatly. Lacan considered that the application of phenomenology to human phenomena could be seen as a challenge to the apparent 'good sense' of scientific method. In referring to the phenomenological method, he wrote in the 1936 paper:

This absence of a fixed reference, . . . this use, which a phenomenological observation makes of the subjective movement itself, and which is eliminated elsewhere as a source of error, seems to sound like a challenge to good method. . . The observer can hide his own personal engagements in the observation he reports to us: elsewhere his intuitive discoveries bear the name of delusions. . . No doubt the paths through which truth is uncovered are unfathomable; you can find some mathematicians confessing to have seen it in a dream, or to have come across it in some trivial collision. But it is decent to present your discovery as though it had proceeded via a route that keeps the 'idea' pure. Science, like Caesar's wife, is not to be suspected.

After all, for a long time the good name of the scientist has not run any risks; nature can no longer unveil itself with a human face, and progress in science has effaced from itself any anthropomorphic character (e, p. 86).

Lacan argued that it was with Freud that a distinction between two methods of research in the psychological field could be identified: 1) a dismissive attitude on the part of medical practitioners towards psychical reality, which was seen as belonging to an imaginary (in the sense of illusory), area; they attributed to the 'real phenomenon of the symptom' only a 'psychological appearance'; 2) an attitude more independent of these prejudices, upon which a new science could be founded, it being no longer deprived of the reality of its own objects of study.

Psychology found with Freud the right to consider its own object – *the psychical phenomenon*. In Lacan's view, Freud broke with the limitations that the science of his day imposed on psychology, and created a shift which seemed to make it fall closer and closer within the range of the human sciences. If one tried to face the more direct and pressing question as to what and where is the psychical material if it is not illusory, Lacan argued, one might then be able to see the links which bind the Freudian description of the human mind to various aspects of these other disciplines.

In order to attempt to answer this question, one has to uncover the sources which make the psychical material known; and then assess the material as it makes itself known. The phenomenological method concentrates on the subject's own account of himself. He is not seen as an object of investigation, but instead as the source of data. New ways of understanding can be found by listening to the subject without preconcepts. To omit what appears unsystematized or senseless in the psychical material would be to lose sight of what might be important.

This approach, said Lacan is very similar to that of psychoanalysis. In the psychoanalytic practice of free association, where the analytic subject aims to say whatever comes to his mind, one sees the rules and conditions of the analytic experience: specifically the two laws of 'no omission' and 'no systematization' of the psychical material. Thus the way that the subject gives an account of himself, with all his hesitations and omissions, his imaginary formations such as dreams, delusions and phobias, and his moments of incoherence, are phenomena which reveal the mental life of the individual. They are what one could call the significant fragments of the subject's life.

Lacan then asked how meaning can be linked with the material which the subject produces. The problem of how to give meaning to phenomena – which seems to be what Lacan meant when he wrote about the 'relativity of the meaning' –

he saw as the nodal problem of the analytic experience. Freud rejected a notion of meaning based on a pre-established system of values into which phenomena are selected and squeezed. Furthermore, Lacan argued, by starting to listen to what his patients had to say, Freud saw in language an irreducible phenomenon of analytic work, and the proper medium of psychoanalysis. (Whether or not Freud took such an extreme position as to situate meaning in psychoanalysis wholly within language is highly debatable, although there is no doubt that he placed considerable emphasis on the role of language, especially in the early years of psychoanalysis.) Lacan then tried to begin to identify the function of language, and its relationship with meaning, particularly in the psychoanalytic relationship. He considered that it is in the awareness of an interlocutor that language starts to have a meaning for somebody: a discourse is always addressed to an interlocutor. There is a phenomenological 'intentionality' in what one says to another person. Even if what is spoken is empty nonsense, there is then the intention to say nothing. There is of course a difference between everyday communicative intentionality and the specific use the analyst makes of it, and so one might say following Lacan that the analyst's function, as a special kind of interlocutor, is to *challenge this role* in a particular way.

The analyst can be left with apparently meaningless language, that is, even when the patient is talking a lot the analyst can be left not knowing what the subject is saying to him. To the question of where then is the meaning, Lacan answered that it is hidden behind what the patient tells the analyst. But the problem that this answer of Lacan's raises is that the listener is supposed to be the interlocutor for the speaker, which would imply that an answer is expected; but then one might well ask what kind of answer is the analytic answer, if the intention is not overtly given, but remains instead hidden? Lacan considered that it is in the movement towards an answer that the listener perceives the meaning, but it is only when he suspends this movement that he understands the meaning of the discourse. He understands it because language in the psychoanalytic setting transmits meaning through its ambiguities, denials and ignoring of intentions.

Once this assumption has been understood, it is possible to look for evidence for it from observation of the experience. In relation to this point, one of Lacan's pupils, Serge Leclaire, described the apparent paradox of the analytic situation in these terms:

> It is no longer surprising today to be faced by the extraordinary situation in which the interlocutor, to whom one refers, seems to have as his only preoccupation that of never showing himself where one would expect him. From the beginning, the psychoanalyst is out of the patient's field of vision, and if the patient finds that the analyst is interested in the subtle Oedipal story he is telling him, his interlocutor only retains the merest hesitations of his language; and if in contrast, the analysand 'offers' the connoisseur a 'choice' slip of the tongue, the psychoanalyst only has ears for the sequence punctuated by the stumble (Leclaire, 1968, p. 18).

Furthermore, when the patient speaks, he solicits in the listener his function of interlocutor, no matter how much the analyst may evade it. One may ask why is it that in spite of the analyst's efforts to refuse this role, the patient's reaction is to implore, insist, challenge and continue to expect an answer, at times producing a monologue? Lacan's answer is that it is this very 'insistence' of speech that the analyst witnesses, in so far as he is also the embodiment of a presence to whom the speech is really addressed. This presence to whom the patient insists on speaking, in spite of the listener's silence, provides evidence for the 'insistence' and permanence of a certain kind of *image*. Howsoever the subject presents this image to the listener, it is certainly human, as it is the cause of passion and leaves behind its mark on the person. In fact this mark (or trace) informs the analyst of the existence of the person's *imago*: the imago is the sum of the various prototypical images which, arising from infancy, remains the subject's more or less fixed projection on the world and others. It is this imago that the patient presents to the analyst in the crescendo of appeals he makes to him, especially in his attempts to blind the analyst and provoke his passion.

Thus the image is an object with a reality of its own and the images which form the imago of the patient are often presented to the 'other-analyst' in a fragmented and diffuse way. They appear and draw attention to themselves at every turning point in a discourse, as well as in the patient's transference relationship to the analyst, e.g., in the patient's memories, silences, periods of forgetfulness and infantile appeals. The analyst cannot escape the function of interlocutor even if this is only as a silent presence. Furthermore, if the analytic situation is determined by a particular kind of dialogue, *whereby the interlocutor is never where he is expected*, it is because the analyst does not pretend to know the patient's truth. Although he is addressed by the patient's words, and so is allowed to assimilate the images and passions the patient imposes on him, he realizes that he is only taking the place of, or listening to what Lacan called the patient's Other (with a capital O), that is, to a discourse which goes beyond the involvement of two people, as we explain in more detail in the next chapter. Lacan placed more emphasis on the need to follow the movements of the patient's discourse than on the need to have an 'immediate', 'here and now' relationship with the patient, although this would presumably not rule out relating to the patient as another subject with whom one can empathize.

The analyst, according to Lacan, will not miss the truth in what the patient is saying if he listens to the patient's Other. In addition, Lacan thought that by considering only the patient's language, one has the possibility of making psychoanalytic discoveries more *formalized*. What he seems to have meant is this: There is a basic 'lack of being' at the heart of the human subject. The subject comes to feel an illusory unity at the time of the mirror stage, but with the introduction of language, he has the possibility of at least representing his thoughts and feelings, including his basic lack of being. Desires and illusions can now be represented in the 'universe' of language. One is no longer lost in some shadow realm of illusions and mirror images, one's knowledge can be tested and formalized. In Lacan's view, therefore, the only way to ensure psychoanalysis a place within the sciences is for psychoanalysts to concentrate on the properties of language. Only through centring psychoanalysis within the study of language can psychoanalytic discoveries became formalized, and so universal.

Lacan ended the paper with a series of pressing questions. For instance: 'through images and objects of interest, how is that *reality*, to which man's knowledge corresponds universally, constituted?' (e, p. 92). He closed the paper asking what 'the research which the Freudian discipline, combining with the new science of psychology, brings to the *reality of the image*, and to the forms of knowledge' (e, p. 92). According to Lacan, Freud had failed to solve the recurring problem of the reality principle, whose objective and universal validity was put in question in the paper. But Lacan left the paper unfinished, and he never presented a promised second part. It was left to the rest of his work to elaborate a more complete and complex theory of the subject, with all his desires, imaginary formations, language and meaning.

II

CHAPTER FOUR

THE ROME DISCOURSE
(1953)

THE ROME DISCOURSE marked Lacan's break with the analytic establishment and the formation of his own school of psychoanalytic thought. Characterized by a markedly polemical style of presentation, it is a manifesto of the aims of Lacanian psychoanalysis. In it Lacan castigated contemporary psychoanalytic theory and practice and proposed a radical revision of the whole psychoanalytic field.

The main thrust of the Rome Discourse pushes for the revision of psychoanalysis by a return to the study of the properties of language, with which the early Freud was particularly concerned. It is a long and difficult text, covering a wide variety of issues, some of which are fully developed, while others are merely mentioned briefly. Anthony Wilden, in *The Language of the Self* (1968), has provided a detailed and quite useful critique of the Rome Discourse; our aim in this chapter is not to cover the Discourse in such detail, but to outline its main points, concentrating on those most relevant to psychoanalysis.

In the Discourse Lacan questioned the main concepts of psychoanalysis and took up issues shared with such human sciences as linguistics, philosophy and anthropology. He believed that Freudian terms could 'only become clear if one establishes their equivalence to the language of contemporary anthropology, or even to the latest developments in philosophy, where psychoanalysis has often only to take back its own' (E, p. 32). In Lacan's view, psychoanalysis is distinguished from other disciplines in that the analyst works on the subject's speech – 'Whether it sees itself as an instrument of healing, or of exploration in depth, psychoanalysis has only a single medium: the patient's speech' (E, p. 40). He pointed out how often Freud referred to language, the proportion of analyses of language increasing when the unconscious is directly tackled. From the birth of analysis, language has been its primary field of action and the privileged instrument of its efficacy, it is the 'talking cure' (SE 2, p. 30).

In the Introduction we mentioned some of the reasons for Lacan's decision to go his own way. The Rome Discourse, which created considerable controversy in both the French and the international psychoanalytic worlds is a revolutionary text, and it suffers from a hectoring tone. One is expected to agree with everything, for example that Freud has been betrayed by his followers, and that Freud even betrayed his own early discoveries, but there is little detailed examination of different viewpoints. However, it would obviously not have caused a stir without its polemical style, and Lacan clearly wanted to rouse analysts from their complacent acceptance of psychoanalytic theory.

In the *Preface* Lacan refers to some of the disputes which led to his secession from the French analytic establishment, in particular to the question of the formation of psychoanalysis and psychoanalysts, and the kind of knowledge that is transmitted. He considered that there had arisen in the analytic community a dispiriting formalism that discouraged initiative by penalizing risk, that the students' independence had been ignored, and that the training had become so authoritarian that the students were maintained perpetually as minors. Overall there was an atmosphere of docile prudence, in which the atmosphere of research was blunted. This was in contrast to the true nature of psychoanalysis, whose complex notions have the effect 'that in no other field does a mind run a greater risk, in exposing his judgements, of discovering his true capacities' (E, p. 32).

Lacan wished to put as a priority the formulation of theses and elucidation of principles to encourage research, and to test out contradictory views. The teacher's prime function was to disengage the meaning from concepts that were being deadened by routine use, by re-examining their history, by reflecting on their subjective foundations, and by establishing their equivalence to the latest research in the human sciences. He considered that psychoanalysts were unwilling to learn from their own method.

As a method based on truth and the demystification of subjective camouflages, does psychoanalysis display excessive zeal in applying these principles to its own organization: whether to psychoanalysts' views of their relation to the patient, or their place in intellectual society, their relationships with their peers, or their mission as teachers? (E✶ p. 34).

Lacan thought that there was an urgent need to re-open a 'few windows onto the daylight of Freud's thought' by a rigorous questioning of the whole field.

This whole enterprise perhaps needs to be put into a French context. The Paris Psychoanalytic Society had become hopelessly rigid and conservative in its theory and practice. In addition it sympathized with the American ego psychology school, which appeared to be putting the role of unconscious impulses into the background, in favour of an analysis of the ego and its defences, and an attitude of social conformism. A similar, and almost equally vitriolic, debate about the role of the unconscious was taking place in England, between followers and opponents of Melanie Klein, which is well described in Hanna Segal's *Klein* (1979). Klein was, like Lacan, accused of betraying Freud's discoveries, but the British society never split, owing to the astute diplomacy of those analysts who did not take sides. In addition, Klein never played around with the timing of sessions, and though she was apparently a difficult personality, she was never a demagogue like Lacan. It was also probably much easier for Lacan to attract a large following in Paris than it would have been for Klein in London. Nonetheless, there are similarities between Klein and Lacan, especially in their strong desire to re-examine the bases of psychoanalysis, and in their emphasis on the importance of the workings of the unconscious; indeed Lacan was never as critical of Klein as he was of the ego psychology school.

The *Introduction* puts forward Lacan's views about how to reorientate psychoanalysis. He considered that a number of changes in aim and technique were due to a terrified turning away from the 'Promethean' discoveries of Freud, particularly as far as the whole area of the functions of speech and language was concerned, or what he called more generally the Symbolic Order. Instead, there had been more interest in the functions of the Imaginary Order, and in the technique of psychoanalysis, and at the expense of the Symbolic Order.

Lacan's notion of the three interacting Symbolic, Imaginary and Real orders first appears in detail in the Rome Discourse, but it is not easy to summarize exactly what he meant by it. Bowie, in his article on Lacan in *Structuralism and Since* (1979, pp. 132-3), writes that, 'Each of Lacan's orders is better thought of as a shifting gravitational centre for his arguments than as a stable concept; at any moment each may be implicated in the redefinition of the others.' Another way of understanding the three orders is by contrast with Freud's descriptions of the mind. Freud's topographical descriptions were useful in showing the science of his time that the mind could be examined in a rigorous framework. Freud's models dealt with a system of localities arranged as strata, leading from a surface to a depth. Lacan's orders are not arranged in this manner, but are instead conceived as different planes of existence which, though inter-connected, are independent realities, each order being concerned with different functions. But perhaps the best definition of the orders is that they are different conceptual categories which aim to cover the functions and activities of the psychoanalytic field. In R.K.'s view, Lacan's use of these terms is highly idiosyncratic, and at times one feels that they can be used to explain anything. In spite of these difficulties, however, one can make out several differences between each order.

The Imaginary Order includes the field of phantasies and images. It evolves out of the mirror stage, but extends into the adult subject's relationships with others. The prototype of the typical imaginary relationship is the infant before the mirror, fascinated with his image. Adult narcissistic relationships, e.g., the close, dual relationship between Aimée and her female friend, are seen as extensions of the infantile situation. The Imaginary Order also seems to include pre-verbal structures, for example, the various 'primitive' phantasies uncovered by the psychoanalytic treatment of children, psychotic and perverse patients.

The Symbolic Order is easier to grasp, being concerned with the function of symbols and symbolic systems, including social and cultural symbolism. Language belongs to the Symbolic Order, and in Lacan's view, it is through language that the subject can represent desires and feelings, and so it is through the Symbolic Order that the subject can be represented, or constituted. The Real Order, on the other hand, is the most elusive of these categories, and is linked to the dimensions of death and sexuality, as we see in chapter 9. Basically, it seems to be the domain outside the subject. The Real Order is 'out there'; it is what the subject keeps 'bumping up against', and it sometimes seems to refer to the domain that subsists outside symbolization, as we explain in chapter 8.

The three orders are supposedly interlinked, each order

depending on the other. In the 1970s Lacan conceived of the metaphor of the Borromean knot to illustrate the three orders. This knot is made up of three interlinking elements. They are so connected that if one element is cut, then the other two are set free.

In the Discourse Lacan criticized the psychoanalytic establishment for ignoring the nature and functions of the Symbolic Order, in particular the function of language, with which Freud was intimate. Lacan stated that if the analyst is unaware of the subtle movements of the patient's discourse, then both analyst and patient will become lost in the shadow-realm of the Imaginary Order, forever chasing the ineffable, like someone trying to grasp their mirror-image. He also considered that the basic terms of psychoanalytic experience – the unconscious and sexuality – had become watered down almost beyond recognition. In addition, he castigated the cheerless and rigid manner in which psychoanalytic technique was too often transmitted. Regardless of some intuitive successes, he considered analytic technique could only be understood or correctly applied if the concepts on which it was based were not ignored. And he stated that it was his task 'to demonstrate that these concepts take on their full meaning only when orientated in a field of language' (E, p. 39).

That the medium of psychoanalysis is the patient's speech follows from Freud's fundamental rule that the patient is asked to put everything he can into words, to say whatever comes to his mind, regardless of how stupid or irrelevant it might appear. However, there is 'no speech without a reply, even if it is met only with silence, provided that there is someone who listens: this is the heart of its function in psychoanalysis' (e, p. 40). The heart of the problem for the analyst is what he says in reply to the patient. The pact between the two subjects, analyst and patient, is established at different levels. The patient comes with all his demands, his expectations, his familiar way of talking, and his way of

THE ROME DISCOURSE (1953)

addressing his interlocutor. He wishes the analyst to reply to his speech at the Imaginary level. At this Imaginary level the patient presents what Lacan called imaginary or 'empty speech' (la parole vide). But instead of the analyst falling in with the patient and becoming an 'ally' of his ego, as many analysts have recommended – and which for Lacan would have meant falling in with the subject's alienated desires – he considered that the analyst should reply on another level, the Symbolic level, where the patient's speech is appealing to the truth, and where there is the possibility of the realization of 'full speech' (la parole pleine).

Lacan argued that if the analyst is not aware that the patient's speech expects a reply, that what the patient seeks in speech is the *response of the other*, his interlocutor, then he will simply experience its seductive appeal and the patient's demands all the more strongly; and, not understanding how speech works, may look beyond speech, e.g., at non-verbal communication for what is going on. The analyst will

> come to analyse the subject's behaviour in order to find in it what the subject is not saying. Yet in order to obtain a recognition of what he finds, he must nevertheless talk about it. He then resorts again to speech, but that speech is rendered suspect by having replied only to the failure of his silence, in the fact of the echo perceived from his own nothingness (E, p. 40).

The patient's alienation, or lack of being, is then echoed in the analyst's alienated reply.

In Lacan's view, speech is the dimension by which the subject's desires are expressed and articulated. It is only when articulated and named before the other (e.g., the analyst) that desires are recognized. It is also only with speech that the subject can fully recognize his history. With the introduction of the language system, the individual can put himself and his past in question – and such questioning is what is peculiar to the human subject. The very fact of language's existence alters the view of the past. The subject can restructure events after they have occurred. Indeed, analytic experience reveals a constant rearrangement of memory-traces by the subject.

One of Freud's basic notions was the need for the full reconstruction of the patient's history. While talking to the analyst, the patient's history is brought to light and this is fundamental in the relief of symptoms. The patient does not simply recount events but 'assumes' his history, i.e., he recognizes it as his own, with all its personal meanings and contingencies. In Lacan's view, only speech can do this – 'only speech bears witness to that portion of the powers of the past that has been thrust aside at each crossroads, where events have made their mark' (E, p. 47).

But what does the analyst do with the two basic types of speech, empty and full speech? Lacan considered that the imaginary relationship between the analyst and the patient's ego, and the imaginary, empty speech which takes its orders from the ego, cannot be eliminated and are always present to a greater or lesser extent. This empty speech demands that the analyst falls in with it. Examples of such demands include appeals by the patient to be 'cured' at once, to love or hate the patient as he was treated by his parents, or seductive appeals for constant reassurance. The analyst can easily be tempted into falling in with the patient's demands instead of interpreting them. Empty speech must be recognized, and interpreted when necessary, but only in order to 'neutralize' it, so as to be able to pick up the more significant elements of the subject's speech. The 'art of the analyst must be to suspend the subject's certainties until their last mirages have been consumed' (E, p. 43).

In some ways, this strikes R.K. as being similar to the analysis of defences, though Lacan would probably have disagreed totally. In such an analysis, the analyst gradually interprets the ways that the patient's ego defends itself against unconscious impulses, before interpreting the unconscious impulses themselves. This would seem to be similar to Lacan's analysis of empty speech, but the difference is in the emphasis given by Lacan to the ego's functions. In no way does he see the ego's defences in terms of an adaptation to reality, so he is against any attempt by the analyst to 'prop up' the ego's defences, in order that the ego can deal better with unconscious impulses. For him, the analyst can only see the ego's activities as alienating. And as we have explained, this leaves out any concept of the ego's protective function.

In Lacan's view, the art and difficulty of analysis lie in understanding which part of the patient's speech carries the significant terms, i.e., which part is full speech. Freud's fundamental rule of psychoanalysis insists that the patient lets go his conscious control so that concealed, unconscious purposive ideas assume control of the current of ideas. It is to such ideas, which *insist* on being heard, that the analyst lends his ears. Thus he 'takes the description of an everyday event for a fable addressed to whoever hath ears to hear, a long tirade for a direct interjection, or . . . a single slip of the tongue for a highly complex statement, or even the sigh of a momentary silence for the whole lyrical development it replaces' (E, p. 44).

The notion of true and empty speech owes something to Heidegger's *Rede* (Discourse) and *Gerede* (Idle talk), although *Gerede*, unlike empty speech, is not a disparaging concept. *Rede*, like the Greek *logos*, makes manifest what one is 'talking about', it lets something be seen, i.e., what the discourse is about. As Heidegger put it, *Rede* is 'the way in which we articulate "significantly" the intelligibility of Being-in-the-world' (Heidegger, p. 204). *Rede* discloses Being, *Gerede* signifies a sort of everyday Being. While *Rede* aims at bringing the hearer nearer to participating in a primordial disclosure of Being, *Gerede* does not communicate in such a way as to allow Being to be appropriated in a 'primordial manner', but communicates rather by 'following the route of gossiping and passing the word along'; *Gerede* moves further and further away from the disclosure of Being and truth.

As Wilden has pointed out (Wilden, p. 202), the linguist Sapir made a distinction between thought and speech which is also similar to Lacan's between full and empty speech, and may help to clarify the latter. For Sapir, thought may be defined as the 'highest latent or potential content of speech, the content that is obtained by interpreting each of the elements in the flow of language as possessed of its very fullest conceptual value. . . Thought may be a natural domain apart from the artificial one of speech, but speech would seem to be the only road we know of that leads to it' (Sapir, p. 15). Full speech is like Sapir's 'thought', while empty speech is like Sapir's 'ordinary speech'.

In another paper, a year after the Rome Discourse, Lacan gave a formula which expresses something of what he meant in terms of the quality of the patient's speech. 'The subject . . . begins analysis by talking about himself without talking to you, or by talking to you without talking about himself. When he can talk to you about himself, the analysis will be finished' (e, p. 373).

In order to complete the concepts of empty and full speech, one needs to take account of the nature of the person to whom the speech is addressed, or the interlocutor, and for this Lacan introduced his distinction between the other and the Other.

We have already explained that for Lacan the subject's truth was not to be found in the ego. Instead it is to be found in another place, which Lacan called the place or 'locus' of the Other (with a capital O) at another level. It is not easily reached, for people fear saying something that might be true. Even if the patient lies, or is silent, or remembers nothing, what he cannot say or remember can be rediscovered elsewhere, in another locality. Freud's basic discovery was that the subject speaks most truthfully, or the truth anyway slips out, when the ego's censorship is reduced, e.g., through dreams, slips of the tongue and jokes. In *The Interpretation of Dreams*, Freud quoted Fechner's idea that 'the scene of action of dreams is different from that of waking life.' Freud described this 'other scene' (anderer Schauplatz) as being that of the unconscious (SE 4, p. 48). Lacan's 'locus of the Other' seems to be equivalent to Freud's 'other scene'.

Freud also showed that dreams and other psychical phenomena had a meaning, and that they conformed to a particular language with its own complicated laws. Lacan described on the one hand the speech which takes its orders from the ego (empty speech) and is addressed to the other (with a little o), the imaginary counterpart, through whom the subject is alienated. On the other hand, he described full speech, addressed to the Other, which is beyond the language ordered by the ego. The subject of this speech is the *subject of the unconscious*, which speaks most clearly in dreams, jokes, etc. Thus, Lacan stated, the unconscious is the discourse of the Other. 'The condition of the subject is dependent on what is being unfolded in the place of the Other. What is being unfolded there is articulated like a discourse, whose syntax Freud sought to define for those bits that come to us in privileged moments, in dreams, in slips of the tongue or pen, in flashes of wit' (E, p. 193).

According to Lacan, the analyst needs to distinguish, in the patient's speech, two registers – he, the analyst, is addressed both as the other through whom the patient's desire is alienated; and as the Other, to whom the patient's true speech is addressed. As with his three orders, Lacan manipulated these concepts of other and Other in various ways, and often at first sight confusingly. We have generally tried to keep to a clinical framework when discussing the other/Other, but there are probably other methods of presentation, for instance with philosophical or literary emphases.

In Lacan's view, it is one of the tasks of language to define the imaginary relationship. Language introduces what Lacan called a 'third term', the Symbolic Order, into the dual relationship between the infant and his image, defining and modifying this dual relationship. Lacan thus laid particular emphasis in the Rome Discourse on the function and independence of the Symbolic Order. For him analysts were above all 'practitioners of the symbolic function', with which they should be familiar if they wanted a solid support for their practice. He described in detail some of the properties of the Symbolic Order, with particular reference to Lévi-Strauss and structural linguistics.

Lévi-Strauss (1963, pp. 31-80) suggested that the unconscious social laws regulating marriage ties and kinship are structured like language. Similarly for Lacan, 'Symbols envelop the life of man in a network so total that they join together, before he comes in the world, those who are going to engender him "by flesh and blood"; so total that they bring to his birth . . . the shape of his destiny; so total that they give the words that will make him faithful or renegade' (E, p. 68).

One could say that the subject-to-be already has a place in the kinship structure before he is born. He is already situated as an element in a complicated, mostly unconscious, network of symbols. It is therefore important to understand the fundamental family relationships that structure the union of the patient's parents, the family constellation, what one could call the subject's pre-history, which helps to shape his destiny and with which he has to deal. As with the words of the oracle that foretold the fate of Oedipus before his birth, there are what one could call 'foundation words' that envelop the subject and help to constitute him in an unconscious structure. But, as with Oedipus, man is often blind to his destiny, and he lives his life like another, ignorant of his history. The driving force behind the Oedipal drama (and hopefully in a less hectic way in analysis) consists in the gradual unveiling of the discourse that founded him, and the blinding truth of which he was ignorant.

To illustrate the early insertion of the Symbolic Order, according to which the subject has to structure himself, Lacan put particular emphasis on his interpretation of an observation made by Freud of his grandson. The child at eighteen months of age associated the appearance and disappearance of a cotton-reel toy, which he alternately threw away and pulled back, with the sounds 'o-o-o', which sounded like the German *fort* (gone); and 'ã' which sounded like the German *da* (there). This game was related to his coping with the disappearance and appearance of his mother. Thus once, when she returned after several hours' absence, the baby greeted her with 'Baby o-o-o-o!'. It turned out that the child in his solitude 'had found a method of making *himself* disappear. He had discovered his reflection in a full length mirror which did not quite reach to the ground, so that by crouching down he could make his mirror-image "gone"' (SE 18, p. 15, note 1). It was by the repetition of this game of presence and absence that the child seemed to cope with his mother's comings and goings, and tried to 'wean' himself from her. Freud pointed out that the game was open to several interpretations. He suggested that the child had turned a passive experience into an active one; also that he had taken revenge by throwing away the reel – 'all right, then go away! I don't need you I'm sending you away myself.'

Basing himself on the linguistic diacritical theory of meaning (see Appendix 1) as arising from oppositions, Lacan commented that in the play of phonemes (o-o-o-o and ã), the child had carried on to the symbolic plane the phenomenon of presence and absence and he was born into language. 'Through the word – already a presence made of absence – absence gives itself a name . . . from this pair of sounds modulated in presence and absence . . . there is born the world of meaning of a particular language in which the world of things will come to be arranged' (E, p. 65).

We have only sketched out some of the ways the Imaginary and Symbolic Orders are supposed to interact, and have hardly touched on the Real. Its place will become clearer in later chapters, in which we also discuss some of the clinical implications of the three orders. For now we will end with a final quote from the conclusion of the Rome Discourse.

> The psychoanalytic experience has rediscovered in man the imperative of the Word as the law that has formed him in its image. It manipulates the poetic function of language to give to his desire its symbolic mediation. May that experience enable you to understand at last that it is in the gift of speech that all the reality of its effects resides; for it is by way of this gift that all reality has come to man and it is by his continued act that he maintains it (E, p. 106).

This quotation summarizes Lacan's fundamental attitude to the role of language and the Symbolic Order: regardless of the presence of pre-verbal structures in the subject and of the role of images, the subject is constituted by the Symbolic Order. The subject's reality is, for Lacan, the reality of the Symbolic Order. A further illustration of this concept can be seen in Lacan's essay on 'The Purloined Letter' by Poe, the essay being an allegory of Lacan's emphatic insistence on the primacy of the Symbolic Order.

Unfortunately there is little discussion, either in the Rome Discourse, or in Lacan's later work, of objections to the idea of the primacy of the Symbolic Order. There is, for example, in R.K.'s opinion, virtually no discussion of the role of visual experience except in terms of the mirror stage. Although it could be cogently argued that the analytic experience is mainly verbal, and should be kept verbal, it seems to R.K. very debatable to extend this notion to all other experience.

Chapter Five

'THE PURLOINED LETTER'
(1956)

L ACAN'S essay on an Edgar Allan Poe short story opened the *Ecrits* (1966). 'The seminar on Poe's "Purloined Letter"' ('Le séminaire sur "La lettre volée"') is a reworking of material from Lacan's 1955 seminar *The Ego in Freudian Theory and Psychoanalytic Technique.*

The subject of the story is a letter, and Lacan traces the effect on the characters as it changes hands and follows a complicated path, its routes and displacements determining the action and destiny of the characters. He used the story to illustrate his theory that 'it is the Symbolic Order which is constitutive for the subject – by demonstrating in the story the decisive orientation which the subject receives from the itinerary of a signifier' (1956, p. 40). The letter, like a signifier, travels in a definite path, which forms a symbolic circuit, or signifying chain (see Appendix 1), cutting across the subjects of the story. The subjects are changed at each turning-point and displacement of the chain, as they lose, receive or search for the letter.

The 1955 seminar was particularly concerned with Freud's notion of the repetition compulsion, which Lacan linked with the 'insistence of the signifying chain'. As this is basic to the ideas of the 1956 essay, we will first briefly describe Lacan's arguments in the earlier seminar.

In *Beyond the Pleasure Principle* (1920) Freud discussed the significance of various observed phenomena. First, that dreams occurring in traumatic neuroses have the characteristic of repeatedly bringing the patient back into the distressing situation of his accident. Then in human relationships there are often repetitions, the perpetual recurrence of the same thing, such as the 'benefactor who is abandoned in anger after a time by each of his protégés . . . or the man whose friendships all end in betrayal by his friend . . . or again the lover each of whose love affairs with a woman passes through the same phases and reaches the same conclusion' (SE 18, p. 22). Finally, he discussed repetition in the analytic relationship, where patients repeat and revive unwanted situations and painful emotions in the transference. They might try to get the analyst to treat them coldly, so that they feel once more scorned, or they find objects for their jealousy similar to those of their own childhood, etc.

It was thus clear that many psychical phenomena could not be explained in terms of the pleasure/unpleasure principle – whereby mental events were regulated by the avoidance of unpleasure (Unlust) or the production of pleasure (Lust). Instead, Freud postulated a principle beyond the pleasure/unpleasure principle – the repetition compulsion, which could override or was independent of it. He considered that the repetition compulsion should be ascribed to the unconscious repressed, and was the manifestation of the 'daemonic' power of the repressed striving for expression, and at times overriding the pleasure/unpleasure principle to which the ego clung.

Lacan then linked the repetition of the unconscious repressed to the insistence of the signifying chain. To understand this, one should remember that for Lacan the true subject was the subject of the unconscious and not the ego, that the subject was in another place or 'ex-centric' in relation to himself. In Freud's terms, on which Lacan based his idea, the unconscious subject was the 'core of our being [Kern unseres Wesens] consisting of unconscious wishful impulses' (SE 5, p. 603). In Lacan's view the core of our being, the true subject, does not coincide with the ego.

Lacan used the word 'insistence' to express the notion of the repetition compulsion, or 'automatisme de répétition': the meaning of the unconscious subject is pressing or *insisting* on being expressed.

   This, he thought, was essential to the analytic experience, where the subject says whatever comes into his head; or as Freud put it, when conscious purposive ideas are abandoned, concealed unconscious purposive ideas assume control of the current of ideas, and it is possible to reach a pre-existing goal by following the drift of an arbitrary and purposeless *chain* [our italics] of thoughts' (SE 5, p. 528). Thus in analysis, the chain of unconscious purposive ideas (or, in linguistic terms, the signifying chain) insists on being expressed and heard, beyond any attachment to a pleasure/unpleasure principle, or the ego's attempts to stifle meaning. As can be seen vividly in the Poe essay, it was Lacan's significant contribution to emphasize the importance for the subject, both inside and outside analysis, of the repetition of a chain of meaning in a symbolic circuit.

The narrator of the Poe story describes how the Prefect of the Parisian police comes to Dupin, already known to the Police for his inspired assistance on other cases, for help in recovering a letter stolen by a Minister D from a royal personage, presumably the Queen. This letter gives the Minister considerable power over her because of its compromising contents, the details of which the reader never discovers. The Prefect plays the classic role of the policeman, familiar to us from the Sherlock Holmes stories, who has unsuccessfully tried all the usual investigations open to him, including a minute search of the Minister's apartment. Dupin, on the other hand, the man who is supposed to know all, retrieves the letter which is lying barely disguised on the mantelpiece of the Minister's apartment. Dupin later gives a long explanation of his method to his friend the narrator, including a discourse on truth and games. He describes the professional,

93

even cunning knowledge which the police used, but which failed to take account of the case, the thief and the meaning of the letter.

Lacan points out that there are two basic scenes in the story – the first, in which the letter is stolen; and the second a repetition of the first, in which the letter is retrieved. The first scene is described by the Prefect to Dupin, and, as Lacan wrote, is 'played as between a deaf man and the one who hears'; the second scene is described by Dupin to the narrator in different terms, taking full account of the register of truth. One can see in these two dialogues, Lacan wrote, 'the opposite use they make of the power of speech'; and it is the contrast between them that helps to constitute the drama. Lacan compared the first scene to a primal scene, a scene of sexual intercourse between the parents which the child observes, or his phantasy of what he observes. Freud emphasized how the primal scene is grasped and interpreted by the child later, when he can put it into words; in Lacanian terms, when he can link the imaginary experience into the Symbolic Order. The amazement and powerlessness of the Prefect confronted by the drama he describes thus have something of the quality of a child who has not been able to grasp the meaning of what he sees, and is still lost in the imaginary experience.

The primal scene takes place, appropriately, in the royal boudoir. The Queen receives a letter when alone, but is interrupted by the arrival of the King. Since the contents of the letter would compromise her honour and safety she tries to hide it, but, not having enough time to conceal it in a drawer, she places it, open but with the address uppermost, on a table, thinking that she is safe. The King, like the police later, sees nothing. The Minister enters, and in Poe's words, 'His lynx eye immediately perceives the paper, recognizes the handwriting of the address, observes the confusion of the personage addressed, and fathoms her secret.' He replaces the letter with one of his own, while the Queen cannot protest as she is afraid of attracting the King's attention. The Minister leaves with the Queen's letter, while she is left with his letter which she is free to roll into a ball.

The Queen is put into a dilemma – she cannot bring the letter to the attention of the King, as an offence against him would involve her in high treason. 'She who incarnates the figure of grace and sovereignty', as Lacan wrote, 'cannot welcome even a private communication without power being concerned, and she cannot avail herself of secrecy in relation to the sovereign without becoming clandestine' (1956, p. 58). Thus, the letter symbolizes her lack of fidelity. But the royal couple is the symbol *par excellence* of the union and pact between the sexes, and hence scandal and abhorrence would follow if the letter's contents were revealed. The Minister holds power over the Queen by virtue of his possession of the letter, and also by the knowledge that the Queen has of him – that, as the Prefect says, he 'dares all things, those unbecoming as well as those becoming a man'. Thus the ascendancy over the Queen is made complete by virtue, in Poe's words, of 'the robber's knowledge of the loser's knowledge of the robber'.

The Minister wields his power for political purposes – by merely possessing it, and by having it close at hand. As Dupin says, '[I]t is this possession, and not any employment of the letter, which bestows the power. With the employment the power departs. . .' The relationship with the letter is thus strange. Its use for means of power is only potential, since it cannot become actual without vanishing in the process. In linguistic terms it is destined to signify the annulment of what it signifies. The Minister is thus totally dependent on the letter if he wishes to exercise power, and the ascendancy which he derives from the situation is not so much a function of the use of the letter but of the role it constitutes for him.

The police search in vain for the letter, using every method available to them. However, as Dupin says, 'They consider only their own ideas of ingenuity', i.e. they fail to take account of the other, their adversary. Their search is patient and professional, but it is not patience and determination which will succeed. 'Had the purloined letter', Dupin says, 'been hidden anywhere within the limits of the Prefect's examination – in other words, had the principle of its concealment been comprehended within the principles of the Prefect – its discovery would have been a matter altogether beyond question.'

The second scene takes place in the Minister's apartment. Dupin describes how the Minister receives him with studied nonchalance – 'yawning, lounging, and dawdling, and pretending to be in the last extremity of ennui. He is, perhaps, the most really energetic being now alive – but that is only when nobody sees him.' The Minister, like the Queen previously, thinks he is safe. Meanwhile Dupin, not deceived, wears green glasses so that he may inspect the premises. When he sees a soiled and crumpled piece of paper on the mantelpiece (the Minister is usually so very tidy) and with apparently diminutive feminine handwriting on it, he knows he has found the letter. The next day he fakes an incident in the street so that he may distract the Minister's attention, and replace the letter with a facsimile, on which he has written some suitably horrendous lines from a play by the eighteenth century French playwright Crébillon. Thus the Minister is unaware that he is no longer in possession of the letter, and his fate is sealed should he try to wield power based on it. And should he open it, he will recognize through the handwriting the hand of Dupin against whom, we are told, he did an evil turn in Vienna (that city by chance later to become the birthplace of psychoanalysis). Through his sadistic revenge and because of the large fee he takes, Dupin has been taken right into the circuit of the letter, except he sees more than the others. Thus, one can now understand how the circuit has taken hold of all the characters.

From the start, this circuit compromised the Queen's

faithfulness to the King, the figure of law and order, and in a sense the whole story concerns how his law has been diverted and *put far off* – the original meaning of the word 'purloined'. The story deals with a letter which has been diverted from its path. But if it has been diverted, then it must have a course proper to it; yet it is unclear to whom the letter is addressed and what is its destination. If it re-entered the order of the law, then it should be returned to the King, but his place entails blindness. Lacan shed light on this whole situation by emphasizing the similarity of the two basic scenes in terms of what he called the repetition of an 'inter-subjective complex', made up of a triad of three positions and involving three subjects – the loser, the robber, and the third person.

What Lacan calls position one involves the third person – the King, and then the police, both of whom see nothing. The position of the King, blind to the truth, reminds one of the blind ego; or in Freud's words, 'His Majesty the ego' (SE 9, p. 150), which feels itself invulnerable and omnipotent. Position two involves the loser – the Queen, and then the Minister. They both see that the third person sees nothing, and delude themselves as to the secrecy of the letter. Position three involves the robber – the Minister, and then Dupin, who both see that what should be hidden is exposed to whoever wants to seize it. The triad of positions is repeated in each scene, but with the various characters changing place.

In the first scene the Minister is the robber (position three), but in the second scene he moves into position two, taking the place of the Queen. She moves to position one, entrusting the search to the police, who are blind. Once the Minister is in position two, he both succumbs to the same fate as the Queen and also takes on almost feminine attributes, for instance by feigning a degree of effeminacy. In addition, in concealing the letter, he folds it inside-out like a glove (the Queen had turned the letter over), and puts on it an address with feminine, diminutive handwriting. Lacan describes how the Minister, as a result of his new position, seemed to be in an imaginary rapport of narcissistic identification with the Queen, familiar from the mirror stage. He plays a game of cat and mouse, or master and slave, founded on an indeterminate imaginary threat, ultimately of death, while he takes on certain of the attributes of the woman, his counterpart. The Minister, also like the Queen before him, thinks he is free from detection. This position means that anyone in it will be

> trapped in the typically imaginary situation of seeing that he is not seen [and will] misconstrue the situation in which he is seen. . . And what does he fail to see? Precisely the symbolic situation which he himself was so well able to see, and in which . . . he is now seen seeing himself not being seen. The Minister acts as a man who realizes that the police's search is his own defence, since we are told he allows them total access by his absences: he nonetheless fails to recognize that outside of that search he is no longer defended (p. 61).

Then, as the Queen had revealed in her behaviour the letter to the Minister, so does the Minister, through his attitude, deliver up his secret to Dupin. As Lacan wrote, Dupin stresses that the Minister's affected attitude is an artifice

> describing behind the bogus finery the vigilance of a beast of prey ready to spring. But this is the very effect of the unconscious in the precise sense that we teach that the unconscious means that man is inhabited by the signifier: could we find a more beautiful image of it than the one Poe himself forges to help us appreciate Dupin's exploit? For with this aim in mind, he refers to those toponymical inscriptions which a geographical map superimposes on its design, and which may become the object of a guessing game: who can find the name chosen by a partner? – noting immediately that the name most likely to foil a begin-

ner will be one which, in large letters spaced out widely across the map, so discloses . . . the name of the entire country. . . Just so does the purloined letter, like an immense female body, stretch out across the Minister's office when Dupin enters. But just so does he already expect to find it, and has only, with his eyes veiled by green lenses, to undress that huge body (p. 66).

We have seen how the subjects of the story have been modified by the mere path of the letter. They are displaced unconsciously during the inter-subjective repetition, and this displacement is determined by the place which the purloined letter comes to occupy in their trio. The letter, a mobile signifier, passes around in a signifying chain, each person unconsciously aware of what is happening. Only Dupin, presumably like the psychoanalyst, seems to be aware, in Poe's words, of the 'simple and odd' consequences of the situation. Thus Lacan emphasizes how the path of the letter as a pure signifier (remember we never know its contents, or precisely from whom it comes) determines the acts and destiny of the subjects.

If what Freud discovered and rediscovers with a perpetually increasing sense of shock has a meaning, it is that the displacement of the signifier determines the subjects in their acts, in their destiny, in their refusals, their blind spots, their end and fate, their innate gifts and social acquisitions . . . without regard for character or sex, and that, willingly or not, everything that might be considered the stuff of psychology, kit and caboodle, will follow the path of the signifier (p. 60).

In Lacan's view the signifier, which is within the Symbolic Order, dominates over the subject. The Symbolic Order can no longer be conceived as constituted by man, but as constituting him, and we have outlined how each subject is transformed by the effects of the signifier. One can also see how speech invests people with a new reality. As Lacan wrote in the Rome Discourse, 'for its symbolizing function speech is moving towards nothing less than a transformation of the subject to whom it is addressed by means of the link that it establishes with the one who emits it – in other words, by introducing the effect of a signifier' (E, p. 83).

In an addition to the Poe essay, Lacan introduced his 'L schema', which summarizes in pictorial form, the dialectic of the inter-subjective relationships, in terms of four basic poles. This was the first of several such schemata.

L SCHEMA

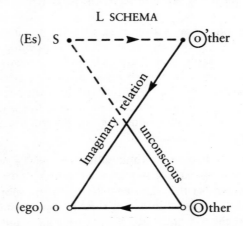

The letter S is the subject – there is a play on words here, as das Es is German for the Id, the unconscious. It is the analytic subject, i.e., not the subject in his totality, but in his opening-up towards his own truth, when he comes to analysis and begins to speak. There are two planes represented here – the Imaginary and Symbolic planes. The Imaginary plane is represented between o and o', the relationship between the ego and its mirror image, the ego's imaginary counterpart, through which the subject is alienated. As we have shown before (p. 58), it is through the form of the imaginary counterpart that the world of objects is constituted. The Symbolic plane is represented between S and O. The Other is the absolute Other (p. 86), to whom the subject's truth is addressed, or who can nullify the subject.

The symbolic realization of the subject takes place between S and O, and is unconscious. The imaginary relationship forms an obstacle to the subject's symbolic realization. What passes between S and O, for instance in the insistence of a signifying chain, always passes through the mediation of the imaginary relationship o – o'. When the subject speaks in analysis, aiming towards the realization of the true subject (when he goes from S to O), he is diverted into o – o'. The truth is thus always being 'purloined', and the subject is constantly drawn to the four corners of the scheme. This duality of symbolic Other and imaginary other is basic to the structure of the subject. As we shall outline later (p. 159), when this duality is suppressed, and the Other as locus of truth is supplanted by the imaginary other, psychosis can ensue.

This schema does not apply solely to the individual but includes the ensemble of social relations, via the Symbolic Order. One needs to understand, Lacan wrote, that 'the psychoanalytic experience runs its course entirely on the relationship of subject to subject, signifying in effect that it retains a dimension which is irreducible to any psychology considered as an objectification of certain properties of the individual.' Indeed the Poe essay is a reasonably clear illustration of Lacan's notion of the Symbolic Order in that he uncovered what he considered to be similarities between the story and the psychoanalytic situation, for example concerning the kind of knowledge needed to discover the patient's truth. In analysis a 'letter' can be found, put aside, diverted or hidden by the patient. The basic analytic task, in Lacan's view, was to find this letter, or at least find out where it is going, and to do this entails an understanding of the Symbolic Order.

Still one reasonable objection to the whole programme of

the essay can be made concerning the letter itself. Lacan was supposed to be emphasizing the power of speech in psychoanalysis, yet he used a written letter as a metaphor of the signifier, and in the Poe essay made relatively little reference to the nature of speech. His point becomes clearer if one considers why he put the essay at the beginning of the *Ecrits* (1966) – it would seem to be telling the reader how to approach the text: by following the path of the signifier.

One is still left, however, with a series of unanswered questions concerning the nature of the Symbolic Order. In R.K.'s opinion, one does not know exactly what Lacan means by the term 'symbolic', or indeed, 'symbol', despite his discussions of other concepts of symbolism. He certainly leant heavily on Lévi-Strauss, who emphasized the world of rules and symbolic relationships into which one is born, and considered that the unconscious is something which imposes form on the world outside. For both Lacan and Lévi-Strauss, the Symbolic Order and the unconscious seem to coincide. Lacan's Symbolic Order appears to refer to a symbolic structure based on a linguistic model made up of chains of signifiers. Lévi-Strauss' symbolic function depends on the law of incest, while Lacan's notion of the Symbolic Order depends on the law of the father (see below p. 133). But Lacan did not give clear boundaries for his concept of the Symbolic Order – he maintained that to define it would amount to a contradiction of his thought, since he refused to acknowledge that the signifier can be permanently bound to the signified. Although one sympathizes with his aim of not being reductive, the lack of conceptual boundaries means (in R.K.'s opinion) that Lacan's thought runs the risk of being incoherent.

CHAPTER SIX

'THE INSTANCE OF THE LETTER' (1957)

L
ACAN'S 'The instance of the letter, or reason since Freud' is one of Lacan's most difficult works, but its text lies at the heart of his theory. At the beginning of the paper, Lacan himself refers to the difficulty of tightening up the text, which was originally given in 1957 as a lecture at the Sorbonne at the request of the philosophy group of the Fédération des étudiants ès lettres (Federation of students of literature), and written up in the same year. He was concerned not to lose the effect of the spoken word of his seminars, with its flow, interruptions and digressions. 'Writing . . . will assume in this essay a factor that makes possible the kind of tightening up that I like in order to leave the reader no other way out than the way in, which I prefer to be difficult' (E, p. 146). There is no question that the way in is difficult.

The text of the lecture and the essay arose from his meeting with literary specialists at the university. He pointed out not only their common interest in psychoanalysis, but that he was aiming to encounter 'the collusion of their common literary qualification [see footnote p. 104], to which my title pays homage' (E☆, p. 147). The essay was, he stated, aimed somewhere between writing (l'écrit) and speech; and also between two kinds of discourse – that of the university and of psychoanalysis, whose continuity and intermingling he stressed. He considered that he was maintaining his concern to find a discourse for the formation of analysts and analysis which did not follow already established laws and assumptions.

Lacan makes an interesting distinction between *training*, where the subject learns certain established rules, procedures and assumptions; and *formation*, where he is concerned about the identity of psychoanalysis. He considered that there had been too much emphasis on training and not enough on formation, adding that Freud consistently maintained a knowledge of literature to be essential in the formation of analysts, 'the prime requisite of qualification for the formation of analysts, and . . . he designated the eternal *universitas literarum* as the ideal place for its institution' (E⁕, p. 147). That is, Freud was always concerned with the kind of qualification that would best aid the formation of the analyst, and he considered that a literary qualification was the ideal kind.⁕ As Freud wrote,

> If . . . one had to found a college of psychoanalysis, much would have to be taught in it which is also taught by the medical faculty. On the other hand, analytic instruction would include branches of knowledge which are remote from medicine and which the doctor does not come across in his practice; the history of civilization, mythology, the psychology of religion and the science of literature. Unless he is well at home in these subjects, an analyst can make nothing of a large amount of his material . . . [Medical knowledge] neither helps him directly to understand a neurosis and to cure it nor does it contribute to the sharpening of those intellectual capacities on which his occupation makes the greatest demands . . . the experience of an analyst lies in another world, with other phenomena and other laws (SE 20, pp. 246-7).

⁕In our opinion the English translator of the *Ecrits* mistranslated the passage we have quoted in putting 'training' for the French 'qualification'. This misses the point, which was to emphasize the kind of *qualification* needed for the formation of analysts.

Lacan was often to have important contacts with universities, which offered him a platform for his ideas away from the analytic establishment. He also to some extent took part in university politics: in the May 1968 revolution, for instance, he was made president of the Department of Psychoanalysis of the University of Vincennes, a major centre of student unrest. The complete history of the Lacanian school's involvement in Vincennes is described in detail in Sherry Turkle's book *Psychoanalytic Politics* (1978); briefly, however Lacan's attitude to the question of psychoanalytic qualification seemed sympathetic to the university student's rebellion against rigid and conservative university establishments, and his emphasis on 'formation', as opposed to the imbibing of pre-established rules, was an attractive mode of thinking to the university reformers.

The Lacanian school had set up a department of psychoanalysis at Vincennes in 1968, headed at first by the sensible Lacanian Serge Leclaire. Lack of assumptions may be all well and good if you are an experienced psychoanalyst, but not surprisingly there were many disagreements amongst the students and staff about whether or not students should be given marks, or some kind of qualification. The whole situation seemed to get out of hand, with chaos in the classrooms. Lacan made a brief but unsuccessful attempt to restore order in 1969; in 1974, he and his son-in-law Jacques-Alain Miller refounded the department. In effect Lacan stepped into the department, declared all its activities null and void, and set up a completely new structure, with new personnel. Lacan imposed his action on the department without consultation – typical of his approach to institutions. In R.K.'s opinion one could describe Lacan's attitude to organizations as delinquent in the extreme, and one wonders why relatively few people ever stood up to him – perhaps because his dictatorial attitude was preferable to unmanageable chaos.

To return to the theme of the chapter. Lacan is suggesting

in 'The instance of the letter' that one of the most pressing questions for psychoanalysis is to find both its own object of study, and also an identity free from its subordination to other disciplines. He thought, like Freud, that the identity of psychoanalysis needed the mediation of other discourses. Lacan argued that if psychoanalysis is to view the subject in relation to his own truth, and if truth has so far been associated in western culture with reason, then it is with the specialists of knowledge and truth that psychoanalysis has to deal. Two such specialists, the philosophers J-L. Nancy and P. Lacoue-Labarthe, have written an excellent, clear commentary, highly recommended by Lacan, on 'The instance of the letter', *Le titre de la lettre* (1973), which has helped us in this chapter to face the extreme difficulty of Lacan's text. This difficulty lies in the way that he used his text, not only keeping to the linearity of writing, but also not passing 'too far away from speech, whose different measures are essential to the formative effect I seek' (E✩, p. 146).

It can reasonably be argued that Lacan was being unnecessarily obtuse, and that it is absurd to mix up writing and speech. Nancy and Lacoue-Labarthe write that they made the experiment of deciphering Lacan's text by following the laws of speech, by deciphering a certain 'metaphorical interplay'. This interplay, according to them, with its own laws, constitutes both the issue and the style of the paper. But one might ask why such an interplay was necessary, and whether one could not, after all, use ordinary prose to express the same ideas. It is clear that Lacan ignored such questions.

Whether one agrees with his approach or not, he demanded that one reads his text as one would a piece of psychoanalytic work, that is, one has to follow the meaning of the text as it unfolds itself, through what he called an 'articulation'. It is through the articulation of a discourse that meaning is acquired, one has to follow both the usual structure of language, and the way that one metaphor leads to another – the 'metaphorical interplay'. Lacan's prose is an elaborate mechanism for multiplying and highlighting the connections between signifiers. Although Lacan's work does not seem to be poetry, there is definitely a poetical element in it, particularly in the way that he plays around with metaphors.

One further preliminary point: The English translator of Lacan has in our opinion incorrectly translated 'instance' by 'agency'. It would be more accurate to restore the old English word 'instance', which is directly equivalent to the French, (and also to the German of Freud, Instanz.) Instance in English means a pressing solicitation, an insistent request, urgency in speech or action, an urgent entreaty; as well as a trial, and the power or jurisdiction of a court, or the court itself, an authority which has the power of decision. The 'instance of the letter', then, has all these meanings. Instance also resonates with its Latin origins in *instare* (to be above), referring to the dominant and elevated position of the letter, its authority and its power to effect decisions. The 'instance of the letter' is therefore the authority of the letter.

The subtitle 'or reason since Freud', an ironic illusion to classical forms, refers to a certain rupture or break in our understanding of the concept of reason since Freud. The difficult 'way in' Lacan mentioned at the beginning of the essay seems to be that one has to abandon the idea of reason as belonging to the positive sciences; nor does it belong to conscious logical or philosophical reason; but to the unconscious. Reason is now the insistence of a meaning, the primacy or authority of a letter which insists on being expressed or heard. The letter marks the subject like a carved Egyptian inscription, it 'pains' in psychosomatic symptoms, it is the language spoken by and in the unconscious. Thus the problem as posed by Lacan was the relationship between the unconscious and reason. What psychoanalytic experience, enriched by the science of linguistics, 'discovers in the unconscious is the whole structure of language. Thus from the outset I have warned informed minds against returning to the notion that the unconscious is merely the seat of the drives' (E☆, p. 147).

There is less emphasis in Lacan's work on the topography of the unconscious (the ego, super-ego and id instances), but more on listening *literally (à la lettre)* to what the unconscious says: that is, to its relationship with language as common to both reason and the unconscious. He defined the term 'letter' as 'the material support that concrete discourse takes from language' (E, p. 147), but it seems that this material support is not of the usual kind. It is, to use Poe's word, 'odd'. The material support is indeed well illustrated by Poe's purloined letter: though the letter is material, it cannot be found by the police looking for it. The letter is treated by Poe himself (although he did not realize it) as a signifier, something which takes its value from representing games of power and intrigue. Although the letter is the material representation of this 'power signifier', it represents an 'odd' kind of material quality because it is only really the *place* where the letter should be, whether or not it is subsequently found. Similarly with the hysteric or hypochondriac – an effect is produced in the body, whether or not the physician can see it.

The letter also designates the structure of language in so far as the subject is implicated in it. He is implicated in language, even before his birth; i.e., there is a *place* assigned to him by a discourse which pre-existed his birth, 'Thus the subject too,' Lacan wrote, 'if he can appear to be the slave of language, he is still more so of a discourse in the universal movement in which his place is already inscribed at birth, if only by virtue of his name' (E☆, p. 148). The subject can enter the inter-subjective field – that is, can enter into the act of relating to others, drawing, from language, the common materials of communication – as long as he is already involved in a common concrete discourse, which pre-dated his birth. One may recall the Saussurian concept of 'la langue' as a system of interrelated items whose value is defined by their place in the langue system, rather than by their history or etymology.

The letter seems to indicate the dependence of the subject, not so much on an environment or a community, but on 'a discourse in the universal movement' which founds the elementary structures of culture. The subject is a slave to the authority of language rather than to society. Lacan was thinking of Leví-Strauss when he altered the traditional opposition of nature/society to the tertiary conception nature/society/culture, where culture 'could well be reduced to language, or that which essentially distinguishes human society from natural societies' (E, p. 148). According to Nancy and Lacoue-Labarthe, Lacan is also referring in the context to Rousseau's Social Contract, with its problem of the conventional passage from animality to humanity.

In the paper, Lacan attempts to look for the foundations of a specific theory of the human subject on the basis of Saussure's foundation of linguistics as a science. One should note that Lacan had a view of science with which many Anglo-American scientists, at least, would disagree. Unlike natural scientists, Lacan was not particularly interested in empirical data, but the kind of logical proceedings and modes of calculation needed to understand phenomena. What guaranteed the status of a science, in his view, was its formalization. The danger of this view of science is that it can become completely divorced from empirical data. In the 1960s Lacan became more and more interested (some would say obsessed) with the application of mathematics to psychoanalysis. But he gave little justification for his pseudo-mathematical formulae, or 'mathemes'. It is certainly true that a discipline may begin to become a science when one can produce basic formulae, or what Lacan called 'algorithms', which can make the discipline more formalized. But one may doubt the validity of trying to equate linguistic formalizations with scientific formulae, as for example when Lacan wrote, 'To pinpoint the emergence of linguistic science we say that, as in the case of all sciences in the modern sense, it is contained in the constitutive moment of an algorithm that is its foundation. This algorithm is S/s, which is read as: the signifier over the signified, "over" corresponding to the bar separating the two stages' (E, p. 149).

As linguistics was founded by the concept of the sign, whose function is to formulate the structure of knowledge, the algorithm S/s is, in Lacan's view, the sign founding all Saussure's teaching. The argument continues by stating that the original Saussurian algorithm was isolated in an ellipse

indicating the structural unity of the sign. Lacan claimed to have upset this conception of the sign by considering the signifier and signified instead as two distinct and separate orders, in a radical opposition; that was why he wrote the algorithm without the unifying ellipse. He introduced what he called a 'cut' (coupure) into the Saussurian sign with the introduction of a new emphasis on the bar, as a formula of separateness rather than reciprocity of signifier and signified.

This new attention to the bar implies a change in the view of the signifier/signified relationship, and calls into question any view which unites language and thing. The primordial distinction S/s 'goes well beyond the discussion concerning the arbitrariness of the sign, as it has been elaborated since the earliest reflections of the ancients, and even beyond the impasse which, through the same period, has been encountered in every discussion of the bi-univocal correspondence between the word and the thing, if only in the act of naming' (E, p. 149).

We suggested in the Introduction that this reversal of the Saussurian sign overturns our notions of knowledge. Gone is the never-ending quest for the concept as such; instead one is left with the available signifier, whose laws must be followed, if one is to uncover knowledge and discover meaning.

Lacan illustrated the way that the signifier and signified occupy different and separated domains as follows. First there is the schema of the tree,

TREE

which, unlike Saussure, has no ellipse or arrows,* and the two different spaces of word and image are bluntly divided by the bar. This is followed by

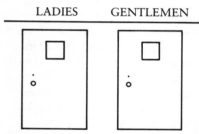

We see that, without greatly extending the scope of the signifier concerned in the experiment, that is, by doubling a noun through the mere juxtaposition of two terms whose complementary meanings ought apparently to reinforce each other, a surprise is produced by an unexpected precipitation of an unexpected meaning: the image of twin doors symbolizing, through the solitary confinement offered Western Man for the satisfaction of his natural needs away from home, the imperative that he seems to share with the great majority of primitive com-

* In Saussure, the ellipse is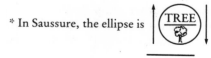

munities by which his public life is subjected to the laws of urinary segregation (E, p. 151).

Thus the signifier is split into the Ladies/Gentlemen difference. The difference in the space above the bar determines a difference in what is below the bar, the twin doors representing the signified, i.e., the law of sexual segregation. The diagram illustrates an image of everyday experience, twin doors with identical handles and plaques, above which one can read the signifier of their sexual difference, Ladies and Gentlemen. And thus the signifier enters the signified in a real way, not 'immaterially'. It is the signifier that does the work of carving out or *articulating* the difference between identical doors. (The only difference between them is the signifier above them.)

To continue the illustration, Lacan cited a childhood memory which the above schema awoke in a friend. 'A train arrives at a station. A little boy and a little girl, brother and sister, are seated in a compartment face to face next to the window through which the buildings along the station platform can be seen passing as the train pulls to a stop. "Look," says the brother, "we're at Ladies!"; "Idiot!" replies his sister, "Can't you see we're at Gentlemen" ' (E, p. 152). Beyond the animal difference of sex, 'destined for the usual oblivion of natural mists', the signifier carries with it the more powerful and long-lasting 'dissension' and ideological opposition between the two children, as they occupy two distinct places which make them look at opposite sides. 'For these children LADIES and GENTLEMEN will be henceforth two countries towards which each of their souls will strive on divergent wings, and between which a truce will be the more impossible since they are actually the same country and neither can compromise on its own superiority without detracting from the glory of the other' (E, p. 152).

The algorithm S/s then contains this separation of the two places, it marks reciprocal positions. In itself, the algorithm functions within the system like a signifier, i.e., it is meaningless in itself. 'It is itself only pure function of the signifier.' And, like the signifier, it has the same *articulated* structure, meaning that each signifier is reducible to differential elements – the phonemes, and ultimately Jakobson's differential features (see Appendix 1); and that signifiers are combined in a signifying chain according to the laws of a 'closed order'. Meaning does not arise in the individual signifier but in the connection between signifiers. '[I]t is in the chain of the signifier that the meaning "insists", but . . . none of its elements *consists* in the signification of which it is at the moment capable' (E✩, p. 153). Lacan also conceived of the signifier as anticipating meaning by unfolding its dimension along the chain itself. One can see this in sentences, interrupted before the significant term: ' "I shall never . . . , All the same it is . . . , And yet there may be . . . ". Such sentences are not without meaning, a meaning all the more oppressive in that it is content to make us wait for it' (E, p. 153).

From what we have described in this chapter and the previous one it should be clear that Lacan affirmed the independence and pre-existence of the signifier, and 'the dominance of the letter in the dramatic transformation that dialogue can effect in the subject' (E, p. 154). For him the term 'letter' refers both to the materiality of the signifier, its ability to be located, and also its differential structure, the fact that it is made up of units of sound which become localized in a structure. This is in contrast to Saussure, who considered that the linguistic sign is the unification of a concept (the signified) with a sound-image (the signifier), and that language takes place between two shapeless masses – the plane of jumbled ideas and the equally vague plane of sound-images. Between these two shapeless masses, Saussure's *Course in General Linguistics* drew vertical dotted lines where the sign unifies the concept and sound-image. He represented a clipping between the two masses, so that signifier and signified are united in one, like the two sides of a sheet of paper. In addition, he described how in time there can occur a shift or sliding (glissement) in the relationship between the signified and the signifier. Thus the Latin *necare*, to kill, becomes *noyer*, to drown. 'Both the sound-image and the concept changed; but it is useless to separate the two parts of the phenomenon; it is sufficient to state with respect to the whole that the bond between the idea and the sign was loosened, and that there was a shift in their relationship' (Saussure, p. 75).

By contrast, in Lacan's view, illustrated in the twin doors example, the two realms of signifier and signified are never united in the Saussurian kind of cut in the sign; there is also an *incessant* sliding of the signified under the signifier. Lacan also disagreed with the exclusive linearity of Saussure's model, instead putting forward the notion that there are 'anchoring points' (points de capiton) at certain important moments of a discourse, when a letter dominates the subject. In order to produce a stable signification at certain anchoring points, according to this theory, the signifier has to stop the sliding-under of the signified. These are the moments of 'tightening up', which Lacan had mentioned at the beginning of the essay. They are marked by a letter which dominates and transforms the subject; they are moments of 'punctuation' in the discourse.

Lacan also stressed that although the grammatical linearity of the chain of discourse is necessary, it is not sufficient to produce signification. The linearity of speech, like the horizontal position in writing, imposes a mainly temporal orientation. But in addition to this horizontal, syntagmatic axis (see Appendix 1), there is the vertical associative, or paradigmatic, axis – 'all discourse is aligned along the several staves of a score. There is in effect no signifying chain that does not have, as if attached to the punctuation of each of its units, a whole articulation of relevant contexts suspended "vertically" as it were from that point' (E, p. 154).

In order to show how words cross the bar at these

moments of punctuation, Lacan evoked the power that words have in poetry, using as an example the word tree – 'arbre' in French, an anagram of 'barre' (bar). We quote the whole relevant passage, which vividly reveals the difficulty of assessing Lacan's work.

> For even broken down into the double spectre of its vowels and consonants, it can still call up with the robur and the plane tree the significations it takes on, in the context of our flora, of strength and majesty. Drawing on all the symbolic context suggested in the Hebrew of the Bible, it erects on the barren hill the shadow of the cross. Then reduces to the capital Y, the sign of dichotomy which, except for the illustration used by heraldry, would owe nothing to the tree however genealogical we may think it. Circulatory tree, tree of life of the cerebellum, tree of Saturn, tree of Diana, crystals formed in a tree struck by lightning, is it your figure that traces our destiny for us in the tortoise-shell cracked by the fire, or your lightning that caused the slow shift in the axis of being to surge up from an unnamable night into the Èv πάντα [All things come from one] of language:
>
> > 'No, says the Tree, it says No! in the shower of sparks
> > Of its superb head'
>
> lines that require the harmonics of the tree just as much as their continuation:
>
> > 'Which the storm treats as universally
> > As it does a blade of grass.'
>
> For this modern verse [by Valéry] is ordered according to the same law of the parallelism of the signifier that creates the harmony governing the primitive Slavic epic as the most refined Chinese poetry. As is seen in the fact that the tree and the blade of grass are chosen from the same mode of the existent in order for the signs of contradiction – saying 'No!' and 'treat as' – to affect them, and also so as to bring about, through the categorical contrast of the

particularity of 'superb' with the 'universally' that reduces it, in the condensation of the 'head' (tête) and the 'storm' (tempête), the indiscernible shower of sparks of the eternal instant (E, pp. 154-5).

Lacan's avowed intent in this essay is to follow the interplay of signifiers, and where necessary this may mean offering a poetical interpretation or presentation. But is this justifiable? One may accuse him of falling between two stools – he is not a poet, yet at times he aims at some type of poetical performance; he is not a philosopher, or linguist, yet aims at some kind of philosophical or linguistic discourse. His answer to his critics was that he was a psychoanalyst, and that he used other disciplines when it suited him for analytic purposes. During an analytic session, one does not ask the patient whether or not what he is speaking is poetry or prose, philosophy or literature. But an additional difficulty in assessing Lacan's work is that he often changed style. He may be giving a series of coherent arguments, and then will suddenly slip into poetry, whimsy, or metaphor. At times it is difficult to sort out whether or not this is valid playfulness, and how thin is the dividing line between playfulness and quackery. Or else one can consider, with Nancy and Lacoue-Labarthe, that the long passage we have quoted demonstrates how poetical interpretation is fused with an attempt to follow the mechanisms of the interplay between signifiers, and the independent production of signification.

Lacan stated that the signifier can only operate if it is present in the subject. The signifier anchors itself to the subject, marking its place with a letter, and *whether or not the subject knows, reads or denies it*, the subject will function like a signified and will always slide under the signifier. Thus the subject is constituted as secondary in relation to the signifier, while signification has a life of its own. 'For what is important is not that the subject knows anything whatsoever. If LADIES and GENTLEMEN were written in a language

unknown to the little boy and girl, their quarrel would simply be the more exclusively a quarrel over words, but no less
ready to take on signification' (E, p. 155).

What kind of subject is Lacan concerned with here, given
the independence of the signifier? We will try to sketch an
answer on the basis of the following quotations, which is
about the function of the subject in Lacanian thought.

> What this structure of the signifying chain discloses is the
> possibility I have, precisely in so far as I have this lan
> guage in common with other subjects, that is to say, in so
> far as it exists as a language, to use it in order to signify
> *something quite* other than what it says. This function of
> speech is more worth pointing out than that of 'disguising
> the thought' (more often than not indefinable) of the sub
> ject; it is no less than the function of indicating the place
> of this subject in the search for the true. I have only to
> plant my tree in a locution; climb the tree, even project on
> it the cunning illumination a descriptive context gives to a
> word; raise it (*arborer*) so as not to let myself be impris
> oned in some sort of *communiqué* of the facts, however
> official, and if I know the truth, make it heard, in spite of
> all the *between-the-lines* censures by the only signifier
> my acrobatics through the branches of the tree can consti
> tute, provocative to the point of burlesque, or perceptible
> only to the practised eye, according to whether I wish to
> be heard by the mob or by the few (E, pp. 155-6).

One may interpret this passage as follows:

If, on the one hand, the subject uses language as a system
common to other subjects, the use he, as subject, makes of it
is to signify something quite other than what he says. His
meaning is then always veering off, or being displaced. This
is particularly clear in the psychoanalytic experience, where
the attention of the analyst is given to this very property of
the signifying chain. One must not then think, according to
Lacan, that speech masks one's thoughts, which, more often

than not are indefinable. It does not mask what we think is true; on the contrary, truth speaks in language as it is continuously produced by speech, through its *communiqué* of facts, in between-the-lines, and at anchoring points. The subject produces through his speech a truth which he does not know about, in Freud's words 'he speaks more than he knows' (SE 20, p. 189). Truth, with its 'acrobatics' on the tree of the signifier, has to be heard and understood. Truth resides, as it were, in the spaces between one signifier and another, in the holes of the chain.

We have to look for the subject within the very structure of the chain, or he is indeed this very chain. He keeps running along the chain of which he is a part, as the signifiers (of which he is made) slide away from the signified, from the 'something'. The result is that the subject's lack of being, or void, his truth, is expressed in this very process. On the one hand, he can be represented by the signifier, but only to be reduced to being no more than a signifier; so that the same moment as he is called to speak, the subject is petrified. It is this process which is summarized in Lacan's definition, 'The subject is what is represented by the signifier, and the signifier can only represent something for another signifier. The signifier represents the subject for another signifier.'

Lacanian psychoanalysis has identified this endless running from one signifier to another (which is the only way for Lacan that anything can be signified) as the linguistic forms of metaphor and metonymy (see Appendix 1). But in Lacan's work, these two 'tropes' or 'turning points' of the discourse are looked at differently from a purely linguistic point of view, because they are seen as the very effect of a 'meaning which escapes its own signification'.

Metonymy refers to the linear syntagmatic connection of one word to another. In metonymy, a 'paradigm', in this case, a linear structure in which one word follows another word according to a given linguistic order, takes the place of the subject's lack of being. In metonymy an original splitting is represented, whereby the order of language replaces the subject's lack of being. It is from this original splitting, that desire for the lacking object arises – the baby can be seen as a metonymic object for the mother, as it represents the phallus she does not have, while the baby itself is this lack (see chapters 7 and 9).

But it is in the game of the passage from one signifier to another in metaphor – where one word substitutes for another word – that desire finds a pathway for expression. Desire runs through one metaphor and the next without dissolving entirely, as in metonymy. In metaphor a signifier substitutes for another signifier only in order to articulate what cannot be said, that is the signified.

In Lacan's view, the signified resides in the symptom, in the sense that the symptom joins in the conversation, slipping beneath a discourse. The symptom resides in the gap between one signifier and the next – or, as when Lacan wrote $S^1 \rightarrow S^2$, here it is the arrow which links one signifier to another; a nothingness, like the arrow, pierces through the signifiers of the subject who speaks.

The symptom is the effect of a compromise, or anchoring point between signifier and signified. The subject's lack of being is not exhausted in a substitution, but finds its realization in the symptom, in which disguise and revelation are condensed. In this sense psychoanalysis is akin to poetry, in which the interplay of metaphors is a major means of encountering unspeakable truth. In poetry, as in psychoanalysis, language is pushed to its limits, and becomes a struggle with the inexpressible. '[T]he metaphoric structure indicates that it is in the substitution of signifier for signifier that an effect of signification is produced that is creative or poetic, in other words, which is the advent of the signification in question' (E, p. 164).

One might say that it is in its function of dismantling language that poetry has to operate, in order to express something beyond ordinary language – whether the effect of creation or revelation takes place as a disturbance, or ineffable enjoyment, or within the highly condensed dream images described by Freud in *The Interpretation of Dreams*.

Lacan's whole teaching is metaphorical. The highly condensed language of his writing leads to the realm of the ineffable, reaching the enigma of poetry, or often just enigma.

> And the enigmas that desire seems to pose for a 'natural philosophy' – its frenzy mocking the abyss of the infinite, the secret collusion with which it envelops the pleasure of knowing and of dominating with *jouissance* [enjoyment, see below, pp. 178-9], these amount to no other derangement of instinct than that of being caught in the rails – eternally stretching forth towards the *desire for something else* – of metonymy (E, pp. 166-7).

Lacan linked metaphor and metonymy to Freud's concepts of condensation and displacement, both essential modes of functioning of unconscious processes. Firstly condensation: one may compare the content of dreams with the dream thoughts. Dreams are brief, meagre and laconic in comparison with the range and wealth of the dream thoughts. The psychical material undergoes an extensive process of condensation in the course of the formation of a dream. Not only are the elements of a dream determined by the dream thoughts many times over, but the individual dream thoughts are represented in the dream by several elements. The construction of collective and composite figures is one of the main ways in which condensation operates in dreams; thus one dream figure may represent a condensation of several personalities. Lacan described condensation as the 'superimposition of signifiers', and compared it to his notion of metaphor, where one word comes in place of another.

Secondly, displacement: one idea's emphasis, interest, or intensity may be detached from it and passed on to other ideas, which were originally of little intensity, but which are related to the first idea by a chain of associations. Thus what appears in the manifest content of a dream as being of minor significance, and barely mentioned by the patient, may in fact be the key to the meaning of the dream. Lacan considered that in displacement one could see a 'veering off of signification', which is similar to his process of metonymy.

Freud considered that displacement and condensation were the two factors basically responsible for the form assumed by dreams. He also considered that condensation and displacement were basic unconscious mechanisms, at work in for instance symptom formation, and the production of jokes and slips of the tongue. The linguistic concepts of metaphor and metonymy occupy a similar place in Lacanian psychoanalytic formulations. Thus the formations of the unconscious, in the Lacanian perspective, derive from the workings of metaphor and metonymy, or what one could also call the play of substitution and combination of signifiers. The dream-work which, in Freud, follows the processes of condensation and displacement follows, in Lacan, the laws of the signifier.

Freud's book *The Psychopathology of Everyday Life* provided a series of examples of psychical phenomena determined by the unconscious. Lacan paid particular attention to Freud's forgetting of the name Signorelli (SE6, pp. 1-7), for it gives a rather clear example of the role of unconscious linguistic processes.

While travelling in the company of a stranger from Ragusa (now Dubrovnic) to Herzegovina, Freud struck up a conversation about Italy. Freud asked his companion whether he had been to Orvieto to see the famous frescos, painted by. . . And here Freud could not recall the painter. He could only produce Botticelli and Boltraffio. Later on, he discovered from someone else that the painter was Signorelli (Signor is the equivalent of the German Herr, or the English Sir or Master). After the event, Freud analysed the forgetting of Signorelli, and the production of the substitute names. He hypothesized that the forgetting was motivated by repression. First of all Freud recalled the topic that the stranger and he had been discussing before the incident, which was the customs of the Turks living in Bosnia and Herzegovina. Freud had told the man that they showed great confidence in their doctors, and great resignation to fate. If one had to inform them that nothing could be done for a sick person, they would say, '"Herr, what is there to be said? If he could be saved I know you would have saved him."' The words Bosnia, Herzegovina and Herr can be inserted into an associative series between Signorelli and Botticelli-Boltraffio.

Close by in Freud's memory there was another remark about fate, told him by the same person who had informed him about the Turks' attitude to death. This second remark was about sexual enjoyment. It was that the Turks placed a higher value on this than anything; and in the event of sexual disorders, they were plunged into a despair that contrasted with their resignation towards death. One Turkish patient had said to Freud, 'Herr, you must know that if *that* comes to an end, then life is of no value.'

Freud had stopped himself from telling his companion about this. He wrote that he had also diverted his attention from thoughts about death and sexuality, for he was still under the influence of a piece of news which had reached him earlier while he was staying at Trafoi. A patient over whom he had taken a lot of trouble had killed himself on account of an incurable sexual disorder. Freud wrote that he was forced to recognize that the forgetting of Signorelli was not a chance event, there was a motive. He wanted to forget events associated with death and sexuality, yet he did not want to forget the name of the artist at Orvieto. His memories associated with death and sexuality unconsciously contrived to place themselves in associative connection with the name Signorelli, so that Freud's act of recall had missed its target. He forgot the name against his will, while he wanted to forget the uncomfortable thoughts intentionally. He then drew a diagram to illustrate how the missing name and the repressed topic of death and sexuality had become linked.

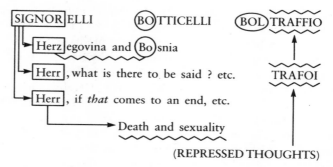

(REPRESSED THOUGHTS)

Freud wished to banish from his mind thoughts associated with Trafoi (his patient), Herzegovina and Bosnia (the Turks). The immediate effect was that he checked himself from retelling remarks about death and sexuality; while the deferred effect was the forgetting of Signorelli. An association connected these thoughts. The word Herr in the two sets of remarks and the first syllable of Herzegovina are associated with Signorelli – Signor being Italian for Sir (Herr in German), as we mentioned above. Both substitute names can be linked with the forgotten name along a series – Signor-Herr-Bo-Trafoi (as in the diagram). Freud suggested, finally, that one could find a deeper link between the names than the mere verbal associations, for the themes depicted in the Orvieto frescos were the four last things – Death, Judgement, Heaven and Hell. Thus another way of looking at the forgetting of the name would be that the word Signorelli itself had conjured up associations of death.

This example reveals clearly that there are mental processes at work which are not accessible at particular moments of consciousness. It also shows that when the repressed returns to consciousness it does so in a distorted, censored form.

Signorelli became distorted into Botticelli and Boltraffio. Freud mentioned similar distortions in dreams and neurotic symptoms. Lacan emphasized that the example also reveals the importance of language mechanisms in repression. One sees the difficulty that the subject meets when he has to say something – there is a discordance between the word for which he is searching (the signifier Signorelli) and the signified (death and sexuality). In addition, the words Botticelli and Boltraffio are in a metaphorical relation to Signorelli (as they come in place of it), as are Traffio and Trafoi. There is also a set of metonymic displacements between the signifiers Signor-Herr-Bo-Trafoi. Finally, one sees in a very concrete way how a person's discourse can suffer from gaps and distortions which are generated by the unconscious, and are intimately related to the person to whom the discourse is addressed – Freud's companion, in this example.

Lacan often cited a joke from Freud's *Jokes and their Relation to the Unconscious* to illustrate further the relationship between the sender and the receiver of a discourse.

> Two Jews met in a railway carriage at a station in Galicia. 'Where are you going?' asked one. 'To Cracow', was the answer. 'What a liar you are,' broke out the other. 'If you say you're going to Cracow, you want me to believe that you're going to Lemberg. But I know that in fact you're going to Cracow. So, why are you lying to me?' (SE 8, p. 115).

Of this joke Freud wrote,

> The serious substance of the joke is the problem of what determines the truth. . . Is it the truth to describe things as they are without troubling to consider how our hearer will understand what we say? Or does genuine truth consist in taking the hearer into account and giving him a faithful picture of our knowledge. . . The joke is pointing to a problem, and is making use of the uncertainty of one

of our commonest concepts (p. 115).

Here, in a few words of Freud, is summarized so much of what Lacan was trying, often laboriously, to say about the nature of truth; though, to be fair to Lacan, he was always at pains to say how often he was merely following Freud.

In the Rome Discourse Lacan described the two basic terms of the psychoanalytic experience as being the unconscious and sexuality. Following the Rome Discourse, he developed his work in these two areas. So far we have described how he reinterpreted Freud's laws of the unconscious. In the next chapter, we describe how he tackled Freud's ideas on sexuality, with particular reference to the Oedipus complex as the anchoring point of psychoanalytic theory. This will be followed by a chapter about psychosis, in which we describe the various distortions to which the Oedipus complex may be subjected.

CHAPTER SEVEN

THE OEDIPUS COMPLEX

LACAN developed his views on the Oedipus complex, which have a very different emphasis from those of Freud, in a series of seminars and essays from the mid-1950s to the early 1960s (see Lacan, 1956-7, 1958). In Freud's writings the Oedipus complex refers to an organized set of loving and hostile wishes which the young child experiences towards its parents. The complete form of the complex comprises both positive and negative versions, in the so-called 'positive' Oedipus complex the child desires the death of its rival, the parent of the same sex, whilst harbouring sexual desires for the parent of the opposite sex. In the so-called 'negative' Oedipus complex the child loves the parent of the same sex, and hates the parent of the opposite sex. According to Freud, the peak period for the experience of the Oedipus complex is at about three to five years of age. He considered that the Oedipus complex played a fundamental part in structuring the personality, and in the orientation of human desires; and that it was basic to psychoanalytic theory and practice.

There have been various modifications of Freud's theory of the Oedipus complex, notably in our opinion by Melanie Klein, who considered that one could detect loving and hating impulses from the early months of life. Klein used the term 'object relations' to refer to her contention that the infant, from the beginning of postnatal life, has a relation to the mother imbued with the fundamental elements of an object relation, i.e. love, hate, phantasies and defences. She believed that the way in which the child dealt with his phantasies and anxieties in relation to the mother's body and the father's penis significantly influenced the development of the Oedipus complex.

The essential feature of the early mother-infant relationship for Klein is that it is the prototype of a relation between two people into which no other object enters. Phantasies relating to the father when the infant is a few months old – phantasies which, according to Klein, initiate the early stages of the Oedipus complex – introduce the relation to more than one object. In addition, Klein distinguished two modes of object relation. In the very earliest months of life, at the so-called 'paranoid-schizoid' position, the infant's impulses are directed towards parts of the mother's body (in particular her breasts) – what Klein called 'part objects'. Since aggressive drives exist from the beginning side by side with the libidinal drives, and are especially strong, the part object in the paranoid-schizoid position is split into a 'good' and a 'bad' object. This is not only because the mother's breast gratifies or frustrates the infant, but also because the infant projects his love and hate onto the breasts.

At about four months of age, with the 'depressive position', a different mode of object relation usually comes into play. The child is now able to begin to see his mother as a whole object, and there is less splitting into good and bad objects – provided there has been adequate mothering, which can modify and metabolize the early anxieties. In the absence of adequate mothering, the infant may have great difficulties in negotiating the depressive position, and its future mental health may be put at risk. But in the 'normal' depressive position the child begins to feel guilt over his hate towards the mother, and fears the loss of her love. At the same time, he enters into the early stages of the Oedipus complex, and turns his attention to objects other than his mother in order to compensate for the fear of her loss. Coinciding with the onset of the depressive position is the gradual adaptation to reality, and an ability to differentiate inner from outer reality. The growing adaptation to reality results in a more secure relation to the external and internal world.

Lacan vociferously criticized any notion of an object relation which aimed at rectifying the subject's relation to the object, or the individual's adaptation to his environment. This was totally opposed to the spirit of Freud's thought, he said, which emphasized the nostalgia binding the subject to the lost object (e.g., breast and mother), and marking the impossibility of his repetitive attempts to find the lost object. Lacan also maintained that Freud emphasized the profoundly conflictual relationship of the subject to the world, so that theories, such as those of the American ego psychology school and to some extent those of Klein, of the adaptation of the individual to 'reality' could be made into a justification for social conformism.

Although many analysts would not deny the importance of conflict in the production of symptoms and in the functioning of the psyche, they would also include an area of mental functioning in the self which is conflict-free. American ego psychology has the notion of a conflict-free portion of the ego, with the ego functioning as an apparatus for regulation of the organism and adaptation to reality. Part of the ego is free from conflict, for example, when regulating many aspects of perception, object comprehension, language, and motor development.

Lacan had a very different view of the ego, as we have already seen. He disagreed completely with any notion of a conflict-free area of the ego or of the subject. These were for him mere illusions, pathetic attempts to keep the divided psyche in some illusory unity. On the other hand, Freud's own ego theory is far from clear, especially as he had no consistent line of thought on the subject. The second topography seems to come nearer to the ideas of ego psychology, although it would be very hard totally to reconcile even his later theories with those of this school. In point of fact Lacan's view of human relations is not Freud's, although Freud did have a somewhat pessimistic view of man's ability to relate to his fellows. Perhaps it would be correct to describe Lacan's approach as an extreme version of one of Freud's many, different and changing viewpoints.

Lacan's particular contribution to this area of psychoanalysis is the emphasis he gives to the function of the *lack of the object*, and *lack* in general. We have several times mentioned his concept of the lack of being engendered by the subject's alienation in the other; he also mentioned a lack resulting from the fact that the subject depends on the signifier, and that that signifier is first of all in the field of the Other. (The infant cannot speak, for instance, but his parents can.) The Poe essay showed how Lacan considered the signifier to dominate the subject, while 'The instance of the letter' showed how the subject is constituted as secondary in relation to the signifier, and how the laws of the signifier impose themselves on the subject. We have mentioned that the fundamental law of the signifier is that a signifier signifies something only in relation to another signifier, and hence that a signifier is that which represents a subject for another signifier. That is, the signifier functions as a signifier only to reduce the subject in question to being no more than a signifier – 'to petrify the subject in the same movement to which it calls the subject to function, to speak, as subject' (Lacan, 1964, p. 207). At the same time as there is the appearance of meaning, there is at another level the subject's disappearance, and there is then a basic division in the Lacanian subject – 'when the subject appears somewhere as meaning, he is manifested elsewhere as "fading", as disappearance' (p. 218). This division also appears in the mother-child relationship and is the basis for Lacan's concept of the Oedipus complex. As he wrote, 'it is in so far as his desire is beyond or falls short of what she (the mother) hints at, of what she brings out as meaning, it is in so far as his desire is unknown, it is in this point of lack, that the desire of the subject is constituted' (p. 218).

In Lacan's reading of Freud, the object is not bound to desire by a pre-established harmony. The Freudian discovery, he thought was marked from the beginning by its concern with desire, but particularly with desire as it appears in symptoms and dreams, where it is problematic. The analytic experience as Lacan understood it, does not reveal a simple relation between desire and an object that will satisfy it, but instead shows how desire is linked in a complicated fashion with the desire of the Other. Hegel had already brought up this latter notion in the master-slave dialectic, in which master and slave strive for recognition of desire and self consciousness through their mutual reactions, but it was Freud, Lacan argued, who brought to light the notion of *unconscious* desire in the relation of the subject with the Other.

In Lacan's view, the object of human desire is the desire of the Other in at least two senses: one can translate the French 'le désir de l'Autre' as both the Other's desire (not mine but the Other's), and as desire *for* the Other. Thus, as the subject's desire is at first unknown to him, he looks for it in the Other, and his desire becomes the Other's desire. The infant early on tries to identify himself with the mother's object of desire in order to be that object of desire, while in addition he has desires *for* her. This basic structure of desire would follow from the law of the signifier, in that it signifies something only in relation to another signifier, so desire is always desire for *another* thing.

In the Oedipus complex as understood by Lacan, the mother- (or parent-) child relationship is not dual (as it is with Klein), but has at least four terms, similar to those we described in the L schema (p. 100), with various interactions between the Imaginary and Symbolic Orders. What is essential in his account is the decisive role of the phallus, as the signifier of what the mother lacks, in the relationship between the parents and their child. He distinguishes between

the penis as an organ, and the term phallus, which is a signifier. The mother attends to the child's needs, but the child
does not enter the triangular, Oedipal relationship (and the
Symbolic Order) merely in relation to the satisfaction of
these needs. The relationship between mother and infant is
also based on the recognition of desire, particularly the
desire of the mother, and it is at this level that, in Lacan's
view, the Oedipus complex is formed.

Lacan's emphasis on the role of desire, the function of the
phallus, and the role of language place his views about the
Oedipus complex much nearer to those of Freud than to
those of Klein. Freud's account of the Oedipus complex
posited it at an age when the child could talk. Klein on the
other hand was concerned to reveal pre-verbal structures. In
Lacan's view, although such structures might be important,
they were not fundamental. In his view, the role of language
(in his terminology the function of the signifier) was of
primary importance. Once the child has acquired language,
however rudimentary it may be, then all the pre-verbal
structures are radically altered to fit in with the language system. It is for this reason that Lacan was not very interested in
the frequent psychoanalytic debates about human development, like controversies over the age at which there is a functioning ego, or at which the infant can think. For Lacan, the
crucial fact is that once the child has the capacity for language, there is a qualitative change in his psychical structure
– he becomes a subject.

This account of the Oedipus complex clarifies some of the
functions of the father, which had previously been rather
obscure. In Lacan's view, the father introduces the principle
of law, in particular the law of the language system. When
this law breaks down, or if it has never been acquired, then
the subject may suffer from psychosis.

A further Lacan's version of the Oedipus complex is that
the infant is bound to the mother, who is herself bound to
the phallus in so far as she does not have it. Various neurotic

symptoms and perversions can be considered as imaginary 'solutions' to the lack between mother and child introduced by the question of the phallus. Lacan delineated three inter-related positions in this version of the Oedipus complex; we will outline the basic core, although there are obviously many variations. In chapter 9, we will use this basic framework for a much more detailed description of Lacan's later ideas on the Oedipus complex.

POSITION ONE

The mother provides the necessary care, feeding and satis-faction of needs, while there is within her the desire for something other than satisfying the infant's desires. The mother lacks the phallus, and desires in the infant something other than himself – the phallus she lacks, the basis of the relationship with her father, and of her own Oedipus complex. The mother desires something apart from attending to the child's needs and cares, for behind her there is the Symbolic Order on which she depends, and also the phallus, which plays the prominent role in the Symbolic Order. The infant is then caught in an imaginary relationship, (or 'lure') with the mother, familiar from the mirror stage, only this time centred on the presence and absence of the phallus.

The infant can take up various attitudes with respect to the mother and the phallus. He can identify with the mother, with the phallus, with the mother as having the phallus, or he can think of himself (or herself) as having the phallus. In position one, the infant tries to identify with the mother's object of desire, the phallus.

The infant's main means of obtaining satisfaction is by identifying himself with the mother's object of desire – his desire is then the desire of the Other. To please her, to keep her love (or so he thinks) he must at one level *be* the phallus. He informs the mother that he can make up to her what she lacks, and he will be, as it were, the 'metonymy' of the phallus, replacing the desired phallus by himself. It is around this lure that the fetishist articulates his relation to his fetishistic objects (such as bits of clothing, shoes, etc.) which are symbols of the woman's phallus in so far as it is absent, and with which he identifies. The transvestite identifies with the phallus as hidden under the mother's clothes – he identifies with a woman who has a hidden phallus.

According to Lacan, the perversions seem to play a never-ending imaginary game, where the phallus is neither completely present nor absent.

> The whole problem of the perversions consists in conceiving how the child, in his relation to the mother, a relation constituted in analysis not by his vital dependence on her, but by his dependence on her love, that is to say, by the desire for her desire, identifies himself with the imaginary object of this desire, in so far as the mother herself symbolizes it in the phallus (E, pp. 197-8).

POSITION TWO

In order to escape the all-powerful, imaginary relationship with the mother, and to enable the constitution of the subject, it is essential to have acquired what Lacan calls the 'name-of-the-father' (nom-du-père) or the 'paternal metaphor', beyond the imaginary other. It is a structure somewhat vaguely defined by Lacan which lays down the basis of the subject's 'law', in particular the law of the language system, first of all by introducing the law of 'symbolic castration'.

Lacan's use of the term 'law' seems to refer to the subject's internal psychical organization. 'It is in the *name-of-the-father* that we must recognize the support of the symbolic function which, from the dawn of history, has identified his person with the figure of the law' (E, p. 67). It seems that the father does not have to be present (i.e., there does not have to be a *real* father) for the acquisition of this vague name-of-the-father. The mother's own relation to her symbolic father may be sufficient. Even if there is a real father present what may be determinant is how he appears in the mother's discourse, how he is mediated by her, and whether or not she values him.

In this second position the father intervenes, either directly or through the mother's discourse, as the omnipotent and prohibiting figure, putting in question and forbidding the desire of the mother (le désir de la Mère), laying down the law and permitting identification with him as the one who has the phallus. He says, as it were, to the child, 'No, you won't sleep with your mother'; and to the mother, 'No, the child is not your phallus. I have it.'

POSITION THREE

On this position depends the 'decline' of the Oedipus complex. The father appears as the one who reinstates the phallus as the desired object of the mother, rather than as the terrifying, castrating, omnipotent father who can deprive her. He prefers her as his object of desire, and he appears as more permissive, giving and lovable. As Freud pointed out in relation to the infantile genital organization, centred on the prevalence of the phallus, there are two categories of being – those who have the phallus, and those who are castrated. The little girl enters the Oedipal triangle as a being not in possession of the phallus, that is, by way of symbolic castration. A solution of her Oedipal situation is that she can *receive* the phallus in phantasy from the father in the form of a substitute, a baby, i.e., she unconsciously receives the baby as a 'symbolic gift', a phallic substitute.

The little boy has to accede to the paternal position, in which he feels legitimately in possession of his own phallus. In Lacan's view, the boy goes from being the phallus to *having* it. But by loving and identifying with the father who has the phallus, in position three, the boy runs the risk of maintaining a feminine and homosexual position in relation to him. Thus the situation is always complicated, with the constant risk of a return to the homosexual position in relation to the father, and the accompanying fear of castration. The male homosexual highly values the phallus in that he wants it in his partner, cannot tolerate its lack, and is usually horrified by female genitals. He also often has a close and castrating relationship to his mother.

One may ask how it is that such a castrating mother leads to the over-valuation of the phallus. Lacan considered that at position two – where the forbidding father intervenes, and where the relation of the child to the mother's desire should be dissolved, when the child can no longer identify with the phallus – the future homosexual child discovers that the mother holds the key to the solution of the Oedipus complex; she 'lays down the law'. This may be the case particularly with a distant father whose messages come to the child only through the mother's mediation, or with a father who is besotted with the mother, and cannot function separately.

Many homosexuals deal with rivalry with the father by identifying with the mother who has laid down the law to the father. The homosexual may thus identify with the phallus, but also with the mother who holds the key to its use, rather than with the father. Turning to psychosis, one may see a 'foreclosure' [in Freud Verwerfung], or a complete failure to recognize, symbolic castration and the name-of-the-father, which results in profound disturbances in the Symbolic Order. With the fetishist, there is a denial [in Freud Verleugnung] of symbolic castration, with a partial clinging to the image of the woman with a phallus. What is looked for in the prostitute is the phallus, but this time the anonymous phallus of all other men.

To summarize the central importance of symbolic castration in the Lacanian version of the Oedipus complex, Lacan wrote that

> . . . the unconscious castration has the function of a knot:

(1) in the dynamic structuring of symptoms in the analytic sense of the term, that is to say, in that which is analysable in the neuroses, perversions, and psychoses;

(2) in a regulation of the development that gives its *ratio* to this first role: namely, the installation in the subject of an unconscious position without which he would be unable to identify himself with the ideal type of his sex, or to respond without grave risk to the needs of his partner in the sexual relation, or even to accept in a satisfactory way the needs of the child who may be produced by this relation (E, p. 281).

Lacan's account (Lacan 1956-7) of Freud's case history of a phobia in a five-year-old boy, 'Little Hans' (1909), illustrates some of these points, especially the crisis produced by the castration complex. Freud's own account is long, so we will comment on a few of the main points only. At the outset we should mention that Freud laid down the general lines of treatment and only once had a direct conversation with the boy although he saw him socially, and met him later when he was a young man; the treatment was carried out by the father, a follower of Freud's who communicated the details to him. Lacan considered that Freud acted as the 'symbolic father' whom Hans lacked, the one who could provide a structure for his (and the real father's) anxieties and questions.

At the age of four years and nine months, Hans, an otherwise bright and cheerful little boy, became afraid that a horse would bite him in the street. This fear, according to his father 'seems somehow to be connected with his having been frightened by a large penis . . . he had noticed at a very early age what large penises horses have, and at that time he inferred that as his mother was so large she must have a widdler [in German Wiwi-macher, or wee-wee maker] like a horse' (SE 10, p. 22).

Lacan pointed out that Hans had a close, 'luring' relationship with his mother, as the father half-realized – 'No doubt the ground was prepared by sexual over-excitation due to his mother's tenderness' (SE 10, p. 22). He would often go to his mother's bed for comfort, without much reaction on the father's part, indeed, he was four years of age before he was moved out of the parental bedroom into a room of his own. His phobia was preceded by anxiety that his mother would leave home. (In fact, his parents divorced a little while after the phobia resolved, and the phobia could be seen as Hans' response to his anxiety about his parents' inevitable separation.)

According to Lacan, the case history plots Hans' movement from the luring relationship with his mother to a new Symbolic Order, by means of his phobia and its many transformations – which was not, of course the usual route for the solution to Oedipal conflicts. For Lacan the major events were:

(1) The imaginary, luring game with his mother, which he repeated with his little friends.

(2) His discovery of the existence of the penis just before he was three years old, and when he now classified the world into beings who have a penis, and those without. He did not yet at this time consciously realize his mother did not have a penis.

(3) When he was three and a half his mother found him with his hand on his penis, and she threatened him, 'If you do that, I shall send you to Dr. A. to cut off your widdler' (SE 10, p.78). Soon after this there was the birth of his sister, of whom he was at first extremely jealous, and then his observation of her 'small widdler'.

(4) His extreme anxiety that his mother would leave, followed by the outbreak of the horse phobia.

(5) The phobia developed by means of 'images derived from traffic [or, in Lacanian terminology, signifiers] . . . advancing systematically from horses, which draw vehicles to railways' (SE 10, p. 84). The fact that the phobia

developed in relation to things coming and going was probably related to his anxiety about his parents' comings or goings, a conflict unresolved at the time.

Lacan considered that the resolution of the phobia occurred by means of a transformation and permutation of signifying elements, the living elements of Hans' myths, by means of which he dealt with the castration complex – the horse, the courtyard, horse and cart, railways, etc. This process resembles the transformation of myths as described by Lévi-Strauss.

> Little Hans, left in the lurch at the age of five by his symbolic environment, and suddenly forced to face the enigma of his sex and his existence, developed, under the direction of Freud and of his father, Freud's disciple, in mystic form, around the signifying crystal of his phobia, all the permutations possible on a limited number of signifiers (E, p. 168).

Hans produced a whole series of phantasies, centred around the problem of his father interfering with his own intimacy with his mother. These phantasies were not mere repetitions but, as Freud wrote, 'steps in a progressive development from timid hinting to fully conscious, undistorted perspicuity' (SE 10, p. 130). Hans was confronted by a new situation – he had not yet mastered the problem of symbolic castration and its accompanying symbolic relations, and he had to take account of symbolic relationships which he had not yet organized. He was still puzzled by the role of the father, particularly what his father did with his mother, nor did he know yet what his mother wanted.

Lacan considered that with the introduction of the signifier 'horse' Hans began, albeit in a pathological way, to confront the role of the father. Freud, acting as the symbolic father, told Hans' father to enlighten him that women do not have a penis. Hans responded to this piece of knowledge with more anxiety, but also by producing a series of imaginary formations – e.g., a phantasy of a giraffe, which he imagined entered his room one night (SE 10, p. 37) – which began the reorganization of his Imaginary order and his entry into the Symbolic Oedipal situation. It was, according to Lacan, the knowledge of the castration of the Other, at the level of the Other, (here his mother – that she was castrated), which instituted Hans' castration complex; rather than any threat that he would be castrated if he masturbated, a threat he rather easily laughed off. Freud continued to act as Hans' symbolic father, particularly in his meeting with the boy, when he told him, 'long before he was in the world I had known that a little Hans would come who would be so fond of his mother that he would be bound to feel afraid of his father because of it' (SE 10, p. 42). From this consultation, 'it became apparent that a possibility had now been offered him of bringing forward his unconscious productions and of unfolding his phobia' (SE 10, p. 43).

The horse and cart, which became one of the themes of his phobia, represented several things. The horse was like his father: 'Certain details of which Hans had shown he was afraid, the black on the horse's mouth and the things in front of their eyes (the moustaches and eye glasses which are the privilege of a grown-up man) seemed to have been directly transposed from his father onto the horse' (SE 10, p. 123). A horse can also fall down – Hans had seen this happen once and Freud related this to his unconscious aggressive wishes, for instance that his father might fall down. He also feared that the whole of his world would fall down at this time. In addition a horse can bite – representing not only the castrating father, punishing him for wanting to sleep with his mother and displace his father, but also the biting feeling that overcame him when he feared the loss of his mother's love.

The horse and cart also represented his father as shirking his responsibility – at one level, Hans wanted his father to be angry with him, and to exclude him from his mother's bed;

but, on the contrary, his father never got angry, and was never bad to him. The loaded horse, as Freud emphasized, also represented his mother's pregnancy when she was 'loaded' with his sister. The phobia in itself managed to keep Hans indoors with his mother, 'harnessed' to her.

Hans himself provided an explanation for his symptoms. He used to play horses with the children at the summer resort of Gmunden. While playing this game, his friend Fritzl hurt his foot, which bled, and he also fell down. Hans thought his symptoms arose 'Because they kept saying "cos of the horse" (wegen dem Pferd), "cos of the horse"; (he put a stress on the cos); so perhaps I got the nonsense because they talked like that, "cos of the horse"' (SE 10, p. 59).

Agreeing with Hans, Freud pointed out that the word 'wegen' (because of, cos of) was

> the means of enabling the phobia to extend from horses on to 'Wagen' (vehicles), or, as Hans was accustomed to pronounce the word and hear it pronounced 'Wägen' [which is pronounced more like 'Wegen']. It must never be forgotten how much more concretely children treat words than grown-up people do, and consequently how much more significant for them are similarities of sounds in words (SE 10, p. 59, footnote 2).

Lacan considered that it was because the weight of the word 'wegen' (because of) was transferred by metonymy to what came immediately after (the horse) that the horse came to assume all Hans' hopes for a solution to his anxieties. Before being a horse as such, it was something that was harnessed to another word, that co-ordinated and bound things. It was thus well chosen to be the centre of Hans' struggles with the problem of how he was bound to his parents and they to him, and to the symbolic relationships he was trying to organize.

We have attempted to illustrate how Lacan's unique contribution to understanding the Oedipus complex consists in his study of the role of the signifier, and then in applying linguistic concepts to Freud's text. Although Lacan's interpretations of the Oedipus complex and the Little Hans case are by no means the only possible ones, they do seem to us to be clinically enlightening, and useful. In the next chapter, on psychosis, we continue to provide a clinical setting for the description of Lacan's ideas.

CHAPTER EIGHT

PSYCHOSIS

THE TOPIC of psychosis is important to psycho-analysis as analysts from Freud onwards have used the extreme pathology revealed by psychotic patients to illustrate and extend psychoanalytic theory. Freud himself however, was sceptical about the possibility of practising psychoanalysis with psychotic patients – he did not feel that they were really reachable. The work of Melanie Klein represented a major breakthrough, for she demonstrated the remarkable connections between early childhood phantasies and the phantasies of psychotic patients. She showed how the infant goes through phases of development which resemble states experienced by psychotic adult patients; and she showed how one could use this knowledge in clinical practice, particularly in understanding the transference of psychotic patients. Although her work has many links with Freud, she considered that she was also extending his ideas into fields he had not explored.

Lacan took a much more fundamentalist view of his relation to Freud, and he considered that there had been a failure to take account of Freud's complicated ideas on psychosis. Freud's understanding of psychosis had been reduced to simplistic formulae, such as how the internal world can be transmitted to the external world in projection. However, a major criticism of Lacan in this context (in R.K.'s opinion) is that he failed to take adequate account of the fundamental revolution in clinical understanding represented by Klein's work. Nor did he try to fully take account of the work of e.g. Winnicott on early parent-infant interactions. Some of Lacan's followers, such as Maud Mannoni and Serge Leclaire have tried to make up this gap, but one still has the impression that the Lacanian school has been rather out of touch with such work. It seems to us that Lacan's ideas on the theory of psychosis are the least controversial and the most easily acceptable of his corpus, although what is lacking in Lacan's work is a more detailed account of their clinical relevance.

Lacan discussed psychosis throughout his work. We outlined the Aimée case in order to give the reader some idea of the world of the psychotic. In his seminar on psychosis (1955-6) Lacan tackled Freud's case history of Judge Schreber, a paranoid schizophrenic who wrote a fascinating account of his illness entitled *Memoirs of My Nervous Illness* (1903). Lacan's essay 'On a question preliminary to any possible treatment of psychosis (1957-8)' enlarged on the ideas of this seminar. In addition, Lacan had discussed the notion of foreclosure (forclusion in French, Verwerfung in German), the mechanism he held to be at the origin of psychotic phenomena, in his essay 'Reply to the Commentary by Jean Hyppolite' ('Réponse au commentaire de Jean Hyppolite', 1956a), based on Freud's 'Wolf Man' case (SE 17, pp. 3-123) and his article 'Negation' (SE 19, pp. 234-239).

It is not easy to bring together the many references to psychosis in Lacan's work, nor are current ideas on psychosis particularly clear. The term psychosis is used in many ways, but in general refers to people suffering from so-called schizophrenia, with hallucinations and delusions; manic depression; various paranoid states; and severe hypochondrial, obsessional, or narcissistic states. Regardless of these ill-defined diagnostic categories, psychoanalytic thinking emphasizes the universal occurrence of psychotic phenomena, just as it does with neurotic phenomena, acknowledging though, that the preponderance varies between individuals.

Common features in these conditions are again difficult to define exactly, but, psychoanalytically speaking (in R.K.'s view), one can see three broad features in psychotic patients:

(1) A particular relation to reality;
(2) A special relation of the subject to his speech;
(3) A particular structure of the subject.

(1) THE PSYCHOTIC RELATION TO REALITY

In his articles on psychosis Freud noted the psychotic's altered relation to reality. The 'imaginary external world' of a psychosis attempts to put itself in place of the 'external world'. (In Lacanian terms, there are altered relations between the Imaginary and Real Orders, in parallel with an alteration in the Symbolic Order). Freud described this altered relation as follows:

> A fair number of analyses have taught us that the delusion is found applied like a patch over the place where originally a rent had appeared in the ego's relation to the external world. . . . neurosis is the result of a conflict between the ego and its id, whereas psychosis is the analogous outcome of a similar disturbance in the relations between the ego and the external world (SE 19, pp. 149-51).

He added, however, that there was no sharp distinction between neurosis and psychosis. 'In neurosis, too, there is no lack of attempts to replace a disagreeable reality by one which is more in keeping with the subject's wishes' (SE 19, p. 187). He further added that in both neurosis and psychosis 'there comes into consideration the question not only of a *loss of reality* but also of a *substitute for reality*' (SE 19, p. 187).

We saw how Aimée's relation to the world was mediated by a delusional structure, with all its intentions and meanings; it was not only that Aimée had lost her sense of reality, but her delusion showed that she had a different and substitute relation to reality, whose meaning needed to be understood. In studying psychosis, Lacan stated, following Freud, that 'the problem lies not in the reality that is lost, but in that which takes its place' (E, pp. 188-9). Lacan emphasized the 'rent' or gap (béance) that appears in the relation of the psychotic subject to the world (as Schreber put it, 'the rent in the Order of the World'), and the nature of the 'patch' which the psychotic subject applies over this gap.

(2) THE RELATION OF THE SUBJECT TO HIS SPEECH

Lacan asserted that the failure to take account of the relation of the subject to his speech had resulted in a failure to understand psychotic phenomena. He illustrated his approach by an examination of auditory hallucinations, the psychotic's voices which converse with him, persecuting or informing him (E, pp. 180-87).

The psychiatric definition of a hallucination is a *perceptum* (perception) without an object – the voices seem to come from outside and impose themselves on the individual without his involvement. But, in this perspective Lacan wrote that, one loses the *subject*'s relation to his voices, and so loses any chance of understanding their significance and the constituting function that the voices have for the psychotic subject. We have seen how the signifier, according to Lacan, imposes itself on the subject, and how the signifying chain bequeathes a meaning to the subject – i.e., how the *perceptum* bequeathes a meaning to the *percipiens* (perceiving subject). We have also seen how, for Lacan, the subject is divided as a result of the law of the signifier. It is thus incorrect to assume a supposedly unifying *percipiens*, for the signifying chain, with its many discrete units or 'voices' imposes its structure on the subject, and so introduces a fundamental division into the subject.

In Lacan's words:

. . . I would dare to lump together all the positions, whether they are mechanist or dynamist, whether they see genesis as deriving from the organism or from the psyche, and structure from disintegration or from conflict. All of them, ingenious as they are in declaring, in the name of a manifest fact that an hallucination is a *perceptum* without an object and asking the *percipiens* the reason for this *perceptum*, without anyone realizing that in this respect, a step has been skipped, the step of asking oneself whether the *perceptum* itself bequeathed a univocal sense to the *percipiens* here required to explain it (E, p. 180).

(3) STRUCTURE OF THE SUBJECT

Lacan put forward a detailed scheme for the structure of the psychotic subject, and it is a transformation of his L schema (E, pp. 193, 194, 212). Briefly, when there is a gap in the Symbolic Order and the place of the Other is deleted or seriously disordered, a gap opens in the Imaginary Order, leading to various imaginary distortions, and also new phenomena in the Real Order, such as voices. The altered structure of the psychotic subject coincides with his using language in various ways: the symbolic moorings of speech may be dislocated and he may speak in a roundabout, fragmented, or confused way, or else in an excessively stylized way in which he is 'spoken' rather than speaking.

Lacan claimed that he wanted to shift the perspective onto the 'properly subjective positions of the patient, positions which all too often one distorts in reducing them to a morbid process, thus reinforcing the difficulty of penetrating them with a not unjustified reticence on the part of the subject' (E, p. 181). He illustrated this shift with a rare clinical example, a case of a young woman who shared a close, psychotic relationship with her mother. The sense of intrusion, which had developed into a delusion of being spied upon, was similar to Aimée's dual relationships with her mother, sister and friends. Lacan saw the daughter, a prisoner of this dual relationship. She had suddenly left her husband and his family, of whom her mother had disapproved. The departure 'rested on the conviction she had acquired that the peasants proposed nothing less, in order to put an end to this good-for-nothing city girl, than to cut her into pieces' (E, p. 182).

When the daughter was interviewed, she told Lacan about various insults to which she and her mother were subjected by their neighbours. One incident involved the lover of one of the neighbours who was supposed to be harassing her mother and herself, and it led to a break in their friendship with the woman in question.

> This man [i.e., the lover of the neighbour], who was no more therefore than an indirect party to the situation . . . had apparently called after her, as he passed her in the corridor of the block of flats in which they lived, the offensive word: 'Sow!'

> Upon which, I, little inclined to see in it a counterthrust to 'Pig!', which would be too easy to extrapolate in the name of a projection which, in such a case, is never more than the psychiatrist's own projection, went on to ask her what she might have said the moment before . . . with a smile, she conceded that, on seeing the man, she had murmured the apparently harmless enough words: 'I've just been to the pork butcher's. . .' (E, p. 182).

The girl was hard put to say to whom these elusive words were directed, whether to the man, herself, or to an absent person such as her husband or mother. The uncertainty of the mumbled sentence came to an end with the hallucination of the word 'Sow', and then its meaning became clearer – its intention was a rejection; she was like a sow who should be cut in pieces like a piece of meat in a pork butcher's, as she feared her family-in-law would do; but this rejection of herself, either as the one who should be cut up, or indeed the one who would like to do the cutting up (e.g., of her mother who kept her a prisoner) was unconscious, and it was unable to follow the conscious intention of the subject. The idea of cutting up was unspeakable, and so she absolutely rejected it. Where her speech might have led to a recognition of her fear, instead there was a gap in the discourse, a gap or hole in the signifying chain. At this place, the word 'sow' erupted from the unconscious and appeared in the real as a hallucination. But the word could not follow the conscious intention of the subject, unless it detached itself from her intention and appeared at the end of her phrase, like this: 'I've just been to the pork butcher's . . . Sow!' Thus to summarize this process, in Lacan's words:

> Thus the discourse came to realize its intention as rejection in hallucination. In the place where the unspeakable object is rejected in the real, a word makes itself heard, so that, coming in the place of that which has no name, it was unable to follow the intention of the subject without detaching itself from it by the dash preceding the reply (E, p. 183).

Such an eruption into the real should be made clearer by an account of Lacan's concept of foreclosure to get to which we have to start with one of Freud's texts.

The 'Wolf Man' case was Freud's most elaborate case history, containing a wealth of clinical and theoretical points. Freud concentrated on the patient's infantile neurosis as it was revealed and reconstructed while he was in analysis as an adult, and the major theme was the place and significance of the infantile factor in the genesis and structure of the patient's subsequent illness when he became incapacitated and completely dependent on other people following a gonorrheal infection in his eighteenth year. For several years however the patient made no progress, until Freud gave him a deadline for the end of treatment, which resulted in the patient producing a large amount of new material, of great significance for the course of psychoanalysis.

He was nicknamed the 'Wolf Man' because of a striking dream which he recalled having at the age of four, and which marked the beginning of his neurosis. In it, he dreamt of several wolves staring at him, with their ears pricked up, paying attention to him. It was through the analysis of this dream, and reconstructed childhood events, that Freud introduced the idea of the primal scene, the scene of sexual intercourse between the parents that the child observes or infers. It was also in this case history that he described in detail the concept of 'after-revision' or 'deferred action' (Nachträglichkeit), which he had put forward in the 'Project' (1895), and which Lacan was later to develop. The primal scene is grasped and interpreted by the child some time later than his original observation of it, by after-revision at a time when he can put it into words.

The Wolf Man's primal scene, which became the nodal point for his subsequent neurosis, was the traumatic event of seeing his parents copulate *a tergo*. As Freud wrote, he

> understood it at the time of the dream when he was four years old, not at the time of the observation. He received the impressions when he was one and a half; his understanding of them was deferred, but it became possible at the time of the dream owing to his development, his sexual excitations and his sexual researches (SE 17, p. 38).

The later activation of the scene 'had the same effect as though it were a recent experience. The effects of the scene were deferred, but meanwhile it had lost none of its freshness in the interval between the ages of one-and-a-half and four years' (SE 17, p. 44). The 'stamping' (Prägung) of the original traumatic event had not been integrated into the subject's verbal system, and was limited, in Lacanian terminology, to the domain of the Real. It re-arose in the course of his progress in his symbolic world, thanks to 'the advance of his intellectual development' (SE 17, p. 109).

Of the many currents in the Wolf Man case, the patient's

attitude to castration and the role of the unconscious castration complex are most relevant to the topic of psychosis. Some years after ending his treatment with Freud, the Wolf Man had a further period of analysis, with Ruth Mack Brunswick, after the outbreak, of a psychotic episode. He was then 'suffering from an hypochondriacal idée fixe. He complained that he was the victim of a nasal injury caused by electrolysis, which had been used in the treatment of obstructed sebaceous glands of the nose. According to him, the injury consisted varyingly of a scar, a hole, or a groove in the scar tissue (Brunswick, p. 439), although there was no objective evidence for such an injury. He neglected his life and work, and became obsessed with the state of his nose. His life was centred on a little mirror in his pocket, which he would constantly use to see the progress of the hole. Brunswick gives a beautiful account of her analysis with him, in which she helped him work through some of the unresolved aspects of his transference to Freud. Among other things, she traced his psychosis to a 'hallucinated castration', i.e., the 'hole' in his nose. It was to an earlier, though similar hallucination of castration, and the Wolf Man's rejection of castration in his analysis with Freud, that Lacan paid particular attention.

Freud traced several of the Wolf Man's symptoms to the influence of the primal scene, in which intercourse appeared to the boy to occur via the anus. This was his first theory of intercourse; two and a half years later, when he was four, and of an age to begin to appreciate both the part played by women and the absence of the maternal phallus, there arose the wolf dream, then a wolf phobia, and then a variety of obsessional symptoms. He rejected the new idea of vaginal intercourse, and the unconscious castration complex (whose details we have outlined in chapter 7), and instead clung to the old theory of anal intercourse. Lacan discussed the nature of this rejection by commenting on Freud's text. Freud wrote:

We are already acquainted with the attitude which our patient first adopted to the problem of castration. He rejected [*er verwarf*] castration, and held to his theory of intercourse by the anus. When I speak of his having rejected it, the first meaning of the phrase is that he would have nothing to do with it, in the sense of a repression [i.e., the rejection (Verwerfung) was not like a repression (Verdrängung)]. This really involved no judgement upon the question of its existence, but it was the same as if it did not exist (SE 17, p. 84).

Thus, Lacan pointed out, Freud used the word Verwerfung to mean a rejection of something *as if it did not exist*, which is quite different from a repression. Freud then wrote that such an attitude to castration was not the patient's final one, and there was evidence of his having recognized castration. But the rejection (Verwerfung) belonged to the 'oldest and deepest current which had not as yet even raised the question of the reality of castration' (SE 17, p. 85). Thus, for Freud, Verwerfung was an older and deeper process than repression.

In Lacan's view, the effect of Verwerfung is 'symbolic abolition'. With the Wolf Man, the reality of castration was not integrated into the Symbolic Order, it was abolished and expelled outside the subject, as if it did not exist. The girl in Lacan's clinical example expelled the idea of cutting to pieces, also a form of castration, in the same way.

Lacan elaborated on the nature of Verwerfung, which he called 'forclusion' (foreclosure in English), by commenting on Freud's article 'Negation'. In this complicated and dense essay, Freud described the function of judgement as being mainly concerned with two sorts of decisions. 'It affirms or disaffirms the possession by a thing of a particular attribute; and it asserts or disputes that a presentation (Vorstellung) has an existence in reality' (SE 19, p. 236). Freud went on to describe how judging is a continuation of the original process by which the subject takes things into himself, or expels them from himself, according to the pleasure/unpleasure principle, i.e., what is good or bad, pleasurable or unpleasurable..

The operation by which the subject takes things into itself is called affirmation (Bejahung), and involves a positive judgement of attributes. Lacan considered that a primary Bejahung is the condition for which something exists for a subject; while foreclosure is the Non-Bejahung disaffirmation, the rejection of something as existing for the subject. The primary Bejahung involves taking in and symbolizing (an introduction into the Symbolic Order); while foreclosure cuts short any symbolization, is opposed to the primary Bejahung, and constitutes what is expelled.

But if something is excluded from the Symbolic Order, what happens to it? Lacan stated that what does not come to light in the Symbolic Order appears in the Real, the realm outside the subject, for instance as a hallucination (e, p. 388). This is revealed in Freud's text, he argued, when after discussing Verwerfung Freud outlined a hallucination of a cut finger reported by the Wolf Man as dating from when he was five years old.

> I was playing in the garden near my nurse, and was carving with my pocket-knife in the bark of one of the walnut-trees that come into my dream as well. Suddenly, to my unspeakable terror (unaussprechlichen Schrecken), I noticed that I had cut through the little finger of my . . . hand, so that it was only hanging on by its skin. I felt no pain, but great fear. I did not venture to say anything to my nurse, who was only a few paces distant, but I sank down on the nearest seat and sat there incapable of casting another glance at my finger. At last I calmed down, took a look at the finger, and saw that it was entirely uninjured (SE 17, p. 85).

The incident was clearly another hallucinated castration. It is interesting to note that the boy saw a 'cut finger' while in a state of *unspeakable* terror. What he was unable to speak about, that is, what could not be symbolized and so remained a 'hole' in the Symbolic Order, appeared in the form of a hallucination in the Real Order. Thus the Real Order is the domain that subsists outside symbolization. It is what is outside the subject – in the case of a hallucination, what has been expelled or foreclosed by the subject. The Wolf Man was unable to symbolize castration, and was lost, as one can see in his description of the hallucination, in the Real Order, in which he could not even make an appeal to his nurse.

Leclaire summarizes the difference between neurotic repression and psychotic foreclosure in the following terms:

> If we imagine common experience to be like a tissue, literally a piece of material made up of criss-crossing threads, we could say that repression would figure in it as a rent or tear, which nonetheless could still be repaired; while foreclosure would figure in it as a gap (béance) due to the weaving itself, a *primal hole* which would *never again be able to find its substance since it would never have been anything other than the substance of a hole*, and could only be filled, and even then imperfectly, by a patch, to use Freud's term (Leclaire, 1957, p. 96).

Foreclosure, then, designates a process which is marked by a radical gap or lack, by a hole in the signifier, which precedes any possibility of repression.

In his essay on psychosis Lacan put forward the proposition that Judge Schreber's psychotic world was marked by a primordial foreclosure of the name-of-the-father, with the expulsion of symbolic castration and the paternal metaphor. We can do no more than sketch some of the themes in Lacan's commentaries on the Schreber case; Schreber's own account of his 'nervous illness' is detailed and complex.

Judge Daniel Paul Schreber, a native of Leipzig, wrote that he suffered twice from nervous disorders. The first time was when he stood as a candidate for election to the Reichstag, the German legislative body. He recovered after a six-month stay at the clinic of one Professor Flechsig, who described the illness as an attack of severe hypochondria. Schreber wrote that this first illness

> passed without any occurrences bordering on the super-natural. My wife felt sincere gratitude and worshipped Professor Flechsig as the man who had restored her husband to her; for this reason she kept his picture on her desk for many years. After recovering from my first illness I spent eight years with my wife, on the whole quite happy ones, rich also in outward honours and marred only by the repeated disappointment of our hope of being blessed with children (Schreber, 1903, pp. 35-36).

Soon after he was appointed as judge to the Supreme Court of Dresden, the second illness began. He dreamt, with distress, that his old illness had returned; then one morning, while in a state between waking and dreaming, he had the idea 'that it really must be rather pleasant to be a woman succumbing to intercourse. This idea was so foreign to my whole nature that I may say I would have rejected it with indignation if fully awake' (p. 37). He soon became obsessed with hypochondriacal ideas, for instance that he had softening of the brain, and that he would soon die. He began to experience ideas of persecution, then hallucinations and an inability to sleep, and was re-admitted to Flechsig's clinic. His memoirs describe the course of events leading up to his first discharge a few years later.

As a result of his unusual experiences, Schreber came to various conclusions about the nature of the world, and particularly about the relation between man and God. It was his description of a 'miraculous structure' (outlined below) which provided Lacan with the basis of his own 'structural analysis' of psychosis.

The human soul, according to Schreber, is contained in the nerves of the body. These nerves have an extraordinarily delicate structure. Some of them receive sense-perceptions, while others carry out the functions of the mind. God is only nerve, not body, and so akin to the human soul. But unlike the human body, where nerves are present in limited numbers, the nerves of God are infinite and eternal. They possess the same qualities as human nerves, but in a degree surpassing human understanding. In particular, they have the facility to transform themselves into all the things of the created world; and in this capacity they are known as 'rays'. God exercised his power of miracles on our earth until the ultimate aim of his creation was attained, with the creation of the human being. Then he retired to an enormous distance, and left the created organic world to itself. In general, he diverted his activity to other celestial bodies, and to drawing up the souls of the dead to Blessedness.

Regular contact between God and human souls occurred, in the Order of the World, only after death. Then a man's spiritual parts, his nerves, underwent a process of purification before being recruited by God to the 'forecourts of heaven' (Vorhöfe des Himmels), an expression given to Schreber by the voices. (Freud pointed out that another meaning of Vorhof is vagina.) Souls that have passed through the purification enter into the enjoyment of the state of Blessedness. In the course of their purification, they learn the language spoken by God himself, the so-called 'basic language', a somewhat antiquated German characterized by a wealth of opposites, such as reward for punishment, poison for food, etc. God himself is not a simple entity, but divided into various realms – anterior and posterior – the latter being further divided into an upper and a lower God. There is thus an

eternal cycle of things which is the basis of the Order of

the World. In creating something, God in a sense divests Himself of part of Himself or gives different form to part of His nerves. This apparent loss is restored when after hundreds or thousands of years the nerves of departed human beings who, in their lifetime had been nourished by other created things and had attained to the state of Blessedness, return to Him as the 'forecourts of heaven' (p. 19, footnote 11).

Throughout the memoirs, Schreber added details to this structure as a result of his experiences, and from information given to him by the voices.

This miraculous structure, however, 'suffered a rent, intimately connected with my personal fate' (Schreber, p. 22), as a result of which the existence of God seemed threatened. Due to inexplicable circumstances, the nerves of living men, when in a condition of intense excitement, could acquire such power of attraction upon the nerves of God that he would be unable to free himself from them again, and would thus endanger his own existence. This happened to Schreber, and it aroused God's instinct for self-preservation (God anyway did not understand living men), and caused Schreber intense suffering. No clash of interest between God and individual human beings could arise so long as the latter behaved according to the Order of the World, but such a clash arose because someone had committed 'Soul Murder' on Schreber. This last term is only vaguely described by Schreber, who writes here, according to Freud, 'with the characteristic vagueness and obscurity which may be regarded as marks of an especially intense work of delusion-formation' (SE 12, p. 38).

The voices at first named Flechsig as the instigator of Soul Murder, an act comparable with the efforts made by the devil or demons to possess souls; but it seemed that the problem could go as far back as the eighteenth century, when 'the names of Flechsig and Schreber' played a leading role. Anyway, Schreber concluded, 'at one time, something had happened between perhaps earlier generations of the Flechsig and Schreber families which amounted to Soul Murder' (Schreber, p. 23).

Another major theme of the memoirs was Schreber's delusion of having to be emasculated, or castrated, and transformed into a woman in order to restore the balance of the Order of the World. There is a tendency, he wrote, innate in the Order of the World, to emasculate a human being (Entmannung) who has entered into permanent contact with rays. At first Schreber greeted this idea with horror, then he accepted it as a reasonable compromise if the world was to be saved. He became convinced that he was possessed of many nerves of female voluptuousness, and that he was gradually becoming transformed into a woman. Freud pointed out that this delusion was clearly a realization of the content of the dream that began his illness.

Schreber, then thought he was intimately connected to God because of Soul Murder, and the excessive state of excitation of his nerves. The two were connected in varying ways, for instance as God withdrew, Schreber felt that a call for help was emitted by those of God's rays separated from the mass, and he had sensations of pain, like a sudden pulling inside his head. Then, over the course of years, there was a 'slowing down of the talk of the voices. This is connected with the increased soul voluptuousness of my body and . . . with the great shortage of speech-material at the disposal of the rays with which to bridge the vast distances separating the stars, where they are suspended from my body' (p. 223). As long as he talked aloud, turned towards God, God had no wish to withdraw, as 'He receives the direct impression of the activity of a human being in complete possession of his senses' (p. 204). Schreber and God were connected through the divine rays, whose nature is 'that they must *speak* as soon as they are in motion. The relevant law was expressed in the phrase "do not forget that rays must speak", and this was spoken into my nerves innumerable times' (p. 130).

Lacan considered that Schreber's delusion deployed 'all the wealth of its tapestry around the power of creation attributed to speech, of which the divine rays are the hypostasis' (E, p. 202). In his view, the defect that gives psychosis its essential condition, and the structure that separates it from neurosis, is an accident in the register of the Other. It involves 'the foreclosure of the Name-of-the-Father in the place of the Other, and . . . the failure of the paternal metaphor' (E, p. 215). Where there should be a paternal structure there is 'a mere hole, which, by the inadequacy of the metaphoric effect will provoke a corresponding hole at the place of the phallic signification' (E, p. 201). (One recalls the Wolf Man's preoccupation with the hole in his nose.) For psychosis to be triggered off, the name-of-the-father has to be foreclosed, that is, it never reaches the place of the Other. One can then understand Schreber's damaging 'Soul Murder', which he linked to the *names* of Flechsig and Schreber, and which was responsible for the rent in the Order of the World. (Schreber was often able to distinguish the real figures of the people around him from what they represented in his delusion, thus he distinguished between the man Flechsig and the 'Flechsig Soul').

God, who had withdrawn to an immense distance, had nerve-contact with Schreber, and thus threatened the Order of the World, or the Symbolic Order. The whole structure of the subject was reshaped as a result. First of all, Schreber had visions of the end of the world, and saw his own obituary in the newspapers (Schreber, pp. 82-85) at a time, according to the medical reports, when he was in a catatonic stupor. This marked the 'death of the subject', preceding the attempt at recovery and reconstruction of his world, and meant, as Schreber later described, that a 'very profound inner change' had taken place in him at that time. Freud described how the end-of-the-world phantasy was the projection of an internal catastrophe, in which Schreber's subjective world (i.e. the Symbolic Order) had come to an end after the withdrawal of his love for it (SE 12, p. 70). This catastrophe was a result of Schreber's special relation to God.

Schreber described God, then, as being impermeable to experience, incapable of understanding the living man, whom he can grasp only from the outside, and closed to the inner world. In Lacanian terms God, as representative of the place of truth, the *locus* of the Other, could not, with Schreber, occupy his usual place. This occurred because of the defect in the paternal metaphor, or foreclosure of the name-of-the-father. As a result Schreber's relation to God, particularly at the final stages of his delusions, is reminiscent of the imaginary, luring relationship familiar from the mirror stage. 'As soon as I am alone with God, if I may say so myself, I must continually, or at least at certain times, strive to give divine rays the impression of a woman in the height of sexual delight' (Schreber, p. 281). He also described how he stood before a mirror when the rays approached, seeing how his breast 'gave the impression of a pretty well-developed female bosom'.

With foreclosure of the name-of-the-father, and an absence of the representation of the subject by the phallic image, the relation between the Imaginary, Symbolic and Real Orders is put out of alignment. Lacan illustrated this with a complex diagram (E, p. 212), which schematizes the structure of the subject at the termination of the psychotic process.

To summarize Lacan's interpretation, Schreber's psychotic illness broke out soon after his appointment to the Supreme Court, where he took his place with the representatives of the law. The phantasy of being a woman enjoying intercourse was later to become a major theme of his delusional world, and this represented the expulsion, or foreclosure, of symbolic castration. Unable to take his father's lofty place and be in possession of the phallus, he identified with and assumed his mother's desire; and thus 'incapable of being the phallus that the mother lacks, he is left with the solution of being the woman that men lack' (E, p. 207).

Schreber underwent various sufferings, including the end-of-the-world phantasy, in which he, as subject had appeared to die. Reality was restored to him, but with gross reshapings of the Imaginary, Symbolic and Real Orders. The place of the Other, where God lies, the absolute Father, was displaced by the uncomprehending father, who was remarkably similar to Schreber's real father, a harsh educationalist (Schatzman, 1973).

This lack of paternal metaphor coincided with an altered relation of the subject to the signifier, represented vividly and concretely by Schreber's attachment to God by means of the divine rays, whose law is that they must speak; and by the various speech phenomena that arose in the Real Order, whenever God withdrew from Schreber.

In general, one might say that, as with Freud, the study of psychosis sheds light on the nature of human reality, which in Lacan's opinion is a function of interactions between the Real, Imaginary and Symbolic Orders. These ideas about psychosis, based as they are on a detailed re-examination of Freud's text, are perhaps also the clearest illustration of Lacan's main aims as a psychoanalyst. He wanted to uncover Freudian concepts that had been deadened by routine use; and to show how analysts had ignored the fundamental concepts because so few had really bothered to *read Freud*, especially in German.

However, the main problem when trying to read Lacan reading Freud is that it is quite often rather difficult to decide what belongs to Freud, and what to Lacan. We have tried to sort this out in our expositions, but even so it is often still not clear in Lacan's work. Lacan's literal attitude to Freud, whilst admirable when he uncovered neglected ideas, such as the notion of Verwerfung, can seem (in R.K.'s view) stifling and unnecessarily rigid. One often has the impression that

Lacan considered himself to be the only original analytic thinker since Freud. This is especially true in his late work from the early sixties onwards.

In the following two chapters, we try to face the later Lacan. We have chosen two topics, the subversion of the subject, and feminine sexuality. In chapter 9, we try to put together his later concepts of the Oedipus complex and the structure of the subject in both a theoretical, and to some extent clinical, framework. Feminine sexuality, the topic of chapter 10, was one of Lacan's last preoccupations. He considered that in this field one came up against the limits and enigmas of current psychoanalytic theory, particularly with regard to the nature of the Oedipus complex in women.

III

CHAPTER NINE

'THE SUBVERSION OF THE SUBJECT' (1960)

L ACAN'S difficult essay 'The subversion of the subject and the dialectic of desire in the Freudian unconscious' (1960) remains one of his seminal texts. It
examines the way in which Freud's notion of the unconscious had subverted the traditional concept of the subject,
and was originally presented at a philosophical conference
on dialectics. It is for this reason particularly, though not
exclusively, concerned with philosophical issues related to
psychoanalysis.

Lacan's willingness to face basic philosophical questions
marks him out from most other psychoanalysts, who prefer
to write within clinical boundaries. His attitude was that
analytic practice cannot be divorced from theory, hence that
in analytic research there is a need to examine rigorously
theoretical concepts, and this implies some dialogue with
other disciplines, including philosophy.

In the 1960 essay Lacan claimed that because of the
dominating role of the signifier in the constitution of the
human subject, one can no longer conceive of the subject in
the terms of positivist scientific thought. The subject cannot
be conceived as a 'signified', an objectively knowable thing.
Instead, Lacan argued, one has to think in terms of a different kind of knowledge, for the subject arises in relation to
desire which is *unknown* to him.

One of the most important discoveries of psychoanalysis
has been the nature and function of unconscious desire, for

example as can be seen in dreams and in symptoms. But Lacan was the first to try to put this discovery within a philosophical context, and to examine the relation between the subject and the kind of knowledge with which he has to deal, both within and outside psychoanalysis. If one accepts his claim that the subject cannot be conceived within a positivist framework, then it follows that the relationship that man has with knowledge must be viewed within a non-positivist framework. Lacan pointed out that positivist scientific knowledge arose historically from consideration of the cosmos and then came down to earth, in what he called the technological 'invasion of the Real'.

The Real seems to include the domain of the inexpressible, of what cannot be symbolized, and to be the Order where the subject meets with death and inexpressible enjoyment (see below, p. 180). It also seems to be connected to nature, as a 'brute external force' that has to be controlled; one can also see how in Lacanian terms, positive science tries to control the Real Order, when technology tries to bring the material world under control. Lacan claimed that psychoanalysis, basing itself on a fundamental split between the subject and the knowledge he has of himself, tries to deal with something that knowledge belonging to the Real can never reach. In this sense, Lacan's ideas are closer to certain branches of western philosophy than to those of an empiricist tradition of natural science, for it was with such philosophers as Vico, Kant and Hegel that knowledge came 'down to earth', and was conceived not as a more or less faded copy of an unchanging reality, but as an effort of the human subject.

Lacan's concept of truth can be related to his view of psychoanalytic knowledge. It is that truth is essentially disturbing, and, as Freud demonstrated, expresses itself in the unconscious. While conscious knowledge is ignorant, the apparently unknown knowledge in the unconscious speaks. *It says what it knows, while the subject does not know it.* In

Lacan's view, the unconscious is the language or form through which this knowledge (savoir) about truth is always and exclusively represented; he considered that the psychoanalyst's task was to decipher a 'structure' in which the unconscious represents itself.

Lacan made an interesting distinction between linguistics, the science concerned with the linguistic formalization of knowledge, and 'La Linguisterie', concerned with the side of language that linguistics has left unformalized. La Linguisterie is the language with which the unconscious is concerned, and which psychoanalysis can decipher at the moments when the ordinary language structure is interrupted, or breaks down as in jokes, dreams and parapraxes. La Linguisterie speaks about what cannot be consciously known, what Lacan called 'La bêtise' (stupidity) – by which he seemed to mean that unconscious truth often appears as unacceptable, or inarticulate, appearing in fragments of a thought, in the odd detail of a dream, or in a slight slip of the tongue; all of which may appear at first sight to be merely stupid and of marginal significance.

Lacan often reported that he was not concerned much with 'pure feelings', or with some ineffable 'thing in itself'. He felt that psychoanalysis dealt with what could be represented, in particular with what could be spoken about. He considered that if one is too concerned with what cannot be spoken about, with the so-called non-verbal aspects of the analytic relationship, then one may miss what is actually verbally available. He thus placed the function and structure of language in the forefront of psychoanalytic theory and practice. And (in R.K.'s opinion) unlike many other post-Freudian analysts, he gave little place to any theory of the affects, or feelings, and the importance of pre-verbal structures. These omissions may seem to represent a denial of much analytic experience; it is equally true, however, that most other analytic schools might be said to practise a denial of the importance of linguistic structures.

In Lacan's view the unconscious is organized, and is not simply a vague, disorganized mass of drives. Organized in the form of a questioning, which he called an 'interrogative voice', it has its own logic, as Freud revealed in his early works on unconscious mechanisms. According to Lacan, psychoanalysis does not deal with feelings as such, but with a questioning of emotional states; that is, it is concerned with their meaning, in so far as they are represented in the unconscious.

Since the early days of psychoanalysis, Freud's ideas about affects have had an important place in analytic work. For example, Freud and Breuer discovered that hysterical symptoms disappeared by bringing to light the memory of the event by which they were provoked, and by arousing the accompanying affect, or emotions, that is, 'when the patient had described that event in the greatest possible detail and had put the affect into words' (SE 2, p. 6). Although psychoanalytic theory later dropped this early cathartic model initially based on hypnosis, when affects were meant to be discharged with their accompanying memories, the concept and place of the affect were not dropped. Psychoanalytic experience went on to show how idea and affect can follow separate paths. The aim of repression, for example, is the suppression of affect, although the accompanying idea can remain in consciousness. Freud considered that 'ideas are cathexes – basically of memory-traces – while affects and emotions correspond to processes of discharge, the final manifestation of which are perceived as feelings' (SE 14, p. 178). He also added, however, that in our present state of knowledge it was difficult to express this difference more clearly. Lacan dismissed the Freudian notions of idea and affect. He rarely discussed the nature of feelings in the way that British analysts conceive them, and for this reason his work can seem over-intellectual, an impression enhanced by his rare excursions into the detailed description of clinical material.

Lacan was interested in the 'logic' of the unconscious, which was different from the logic of the ego. This logic appears in the analytic relationship when the analyst finds himself listening to different orders in a discourse – orders belonging to the ego, and to the unconscious. Thus in the sentence, 'I think I do not exist' – the first 'I' indicates the subject of the enunciation (énonciation, the act of speaking the words) but does not signify the subject's existence, which is considered in the 'I' of the statement (énoncé), 'I do not exist'. One is faced here with what Lacan called a 'cut' (coupure), between different orders of discourse – where on the one hand the subject enunciates his symbolic existence as the 'I' who speaks and thinks, but then denies this existence at the level of the statement, 'I do not exist'.

Lacan pointed out that in psychosis the patient often experiences voices that utter interrupted phrases, e.g., 'Now I will . . . myself . . . as for you, you ought to . . . I will certainly. . .' (E, p. 186). Such interrupted statements are not meaningless; for, as psychoanalysis emphasizes, it is at such interrupted moments, when meaning stumbles, where there may be a missing 'letter', when there is a break in the ego's cohesion, that one may recognize the presence of desire (Wunsch in German, wish in English), and the subject's truth.

Lacan considered that since psychoanalysis had discovered articulation and representation in the unconscious, the subject could no longer be considered as merely 'pure existence without being', a being trapped in an inarticulable primary experience. Rather the subject is like the questioner of the tarot, who has to question the reader of the tarot cards before he can know the meaning of his own destiny lying before him. The subject is the one who has to question somebody else, an Other, in order to know the truth about himself – whether this Other be magician, sphinx, analyst, his own master or slave. This questioning may arise, for example, when all the subject's 'sensible' discourse is suddenly interrupted, and signifier and signified are revealed in their separateness. The subject comes into being at this point, when he experiences a lack of cohesion, a moment of 'discord' (cf. the 'mirror stage'), where his own words and knowledge of himself fade away.

This is how Lacan interpreted and translated Freud's 'pre-Socratic' phrase *'Wo Es war, soll Ich werden'*, which has been clumsily translated into English as 'Where id was, there ego shall be' (SE 22, p. 80). Lacan made the valid point that if Freud meant Es to be id, he would have used *das* Es, and similarly *das* Ich for the ego. Instead, Lacan interestingly thought that the phrase has a more subtle and sublime meaning – so *there where It* (the subject, devoid of any *das* or objectifying article) *was, so must I come to being*. Or, in Lacan's words, 'There where it was just now, there where it was for a while, between an extinction that is still glowing and a birth that is retarded, "I" can come into being and disappear from what I say' (E, p. 300).

The Lacanian view of the unconscious plays around with the philosophical problem of ontology, the study of 'being' and 'non-being'. It would seem that, for Lacan, the problem of being cannot be separated from the relation of the subject to the Other. In addition, the Lacanian view of the unconscious revolves around the question of lack, in particular the lack of being that results from the subject's dependence on the Other. One can see certain similarities between the Lacanian concept of lack of being and the Freudian theory of the death drive, which aims to bring the living being back to the inorganic state (SE 17, p. 38). In Lacan's words,

> From the approach that we have indicated, the reader should recognize in the metaphor of the return to the inanimate (which Freud applies to every living body) that margin beyond life that language gives to the human being by virtue of the fact that he speaks, and which is precisely that in which such a being places in the position

of a signifier, not only those parts of his body that are exchangeable, but this body itself (E, p. 301).

In Lacan's view, language represents that 'margin beyond life' where the being of the individual is *only represented*. He considered that the subject is always caught up in language's function of representing something inaccessible, the margin beyond life, and the ultimate, inaccessible experience of death.

Lacan illustrated the relationship between the subject and his death with a dream referred to by Freud.

> A man who had once nursed his father through a long and painful mortal illness told me that in the months follow-ing his father's death he had repeatedly dreamt that *his father was alive once more and that he was talking to him in his usual way. But he felt it exceedingly painful that his father had really died, only without knowing it* (SE 12, p. 225).

For Freud this nonsensical dream could be understood by adding 'as the dreamer wished' after the words 'that his father had really died', and by further adding 'that he (the dreamer) wished it' to the last words. That is, the dream-thought runs, 'It was a painful memory for him that he had been obliged to wish for his father's death (as a release) while he was still alive, and how terrible it would have been if his father had had any suspicion of it!' (SE 12, p. 225).

Lacan examined the sentence, 'He did not know that he was dead.' The dead father would seem to survive only because he is not told the truth of which he is unaware, i.e., the son's death-wishes. One could say that the dead father represents the subject's ego. The enunciation 'He did not know' would then refer to the ego. But what, Lacan asked, does the ego not know? His answer was that the ego is dead. According to him, the ego is caught in its negative function, as it can only exist if it does not know the truth, i.e., that it, the ego, does not exist, and that the subject as ego is 'barred' to his own existence, but not his actual existence; the former is represented in the dream by death, as the ego is only an imaginary representation of the subject. As Lacan wrote:

> If the figure of the dead father survives only by virtue of the fact that one does not tell him the truth of which he is unaware, what, then, is to be said of the *I* on which this survival depends? He did not know. A little more and he'd have known. Oh! let's hope that never happens! Rather than have him know, *I*'d die. Yes, that's how *I* get there, where it was: who knew, then, that *I* was dead? . . . Being of non-being, that is how *I* as subject comes on the scene. . . (E, p. 300).

It seems then that once the signifying chain has marked the subject, death has entered his life. As Safouan, one of Lacan's followers, wrote, 'Only man who "lives in language" can construct the dwelling we call a sepulchre. . . All love includes a death wish . . . a wish that one could describe . . . as a wish to return to the *inanimate state that the subject was as signifier before he was born*' (Safouan, 1979, p. 81).

One might be tempted to restore the 'total' or 'unified' reality of the subject by counting on the concrete reality of the body; but Lacan considered that even this can be contested, merely by reference to the body in psychotic states of disintegration; or the hysterical and hypochondriacal bodily symptoms, which follow no medical reality; or the body of the infant before it is unified in the mirror image. We have already described how the body is *a unity only as an image*: its unity is, from the beginning of life, a function of the signifier and so is its meaning – for instance as a unity it can function as an imaginary 'coat-of-arms' of the body, or as the 'battlefield' of conflicts in a variety of symptoms. One could say that the body always obeys the law of desire.

Lacan's concept of drive underlies his theory of desire. The English term drive translates the German Trieb, and the usual French equivalent is pulsion. Lacan also proposed the word dérive, which corresponds to adrift, in the sense of something adrift, being dragged by currents and not knowing where it is going. This corresponds more faithfully to Lacan's notion of drive, which is not based exclusively on physiology (nor was Freud's Trieb), but on the 'drifting' movement of desire. This movement has available a 'natural' knowledge (savoir in French, Wissen in German) bound to human needs; but the subject still does not know where the current is going and so does not have what is called connaissance in French or Kenntnis in German.

Unfortunately, English does not have distinct words for connaissance and savoir, translating both as knowledge. In this context one could see connaissance as knowledge according to traditional positivist thought, while for Lacan savoir is unconscious knowledge, the special domain of psychoanalysis. As he wrote,

> it is a question of something quite different, which is a savoir, certainly, but one that involves not the least connaissance, in that it is inscribed in a discourse of which, like the 'messenger-slave' of ancient usage, the subject who carries under his hair the codicil that condemns him to death knows neither the meaning nor the text, nor in what language it is written, nor even that it had been tattooed on his shaven scalp as he slept (E, p. 302).

This seems to mean that the mark that is hidden from the subject is what distinguishes him and makes him recognizable, if not to himself, then to others. In this way, the Other becomes the real witness and guarantor of the subject's existence, as it is he who can recognize the subject.

Thus the basic ontological question, which concerns the nature of the subject's being, leads to considering the subject's basic dependence on the Other. This Other is not affected by the same lack as the subject, and can be identified with the mother's original role in relation to the infant. The mother looks after the infant, loves or rejects him, calls him by a name and tells him who he is. She is the 'M-Other' who created him. The Other is the 'place' where the subject is born, not only as a biological entity, but as a subject with a human existence. The Other who was there before the subject's birth, as 'absolute being', is the one who can recognize and love him. But then this very mother, who makes such efforts to care for her infant, who seems to give as much as she can, is also a subject, itself based on a lack of being. The mother's love cannot be absolute as she cannot fulfil this absolute *demand* for love made by the infant. No matter how much she gives him and how much his *needs* are satisfied, the mother can never fill the void she shares with her child. She is never perfect. The demand for love goes *beyond* the objects that satisfy need. In Lacan's view it is in this irreducible 'beyond' of demand that desire is constituted.

> Desire takes shape in the margin in which demand is torn apart from need: this margin being that which is opened up by demand, the appeal of which can be unconditional only in regard to the Other, under the form of a possible defect, which need may introduce into it, of having no universal satisfaction (what is called 'anguish' [angoisse in Lacan's original]) (E*, p. 311).

Anguish arises when the Other, whom the subject had supposed to be faultless, onto whom he had pinned his demands as the unique creator of his existence, to whom he had become subjected, cannot fulfil his absolute demand for perfection.

Thus the subject is subjected to, and alienated by the mother, as represented by the phantasy of her omnipotence, which could be put into words as, 'She does not lack anything, she knows what she wants, and she knows what I want.' There is no need or demand which will confirm this phantasy, whatever attempts are made to fulfil it by the Other – mother, society, or teachers. The lack remains, beyond any fulfilling attitude on the part of the environment. The Other *cannot* be fulfilling, and will never exhaust the subject's appeal for being. The Other, who is supposedly giving the subject everything, is deceiving him, and this produces anguish in him. That is why the psychoanalyst's function is not to answer the subject's appeals and demands, but instead to act so that the answer comes back to the subject from the analyst as a question – 'What do you want from me?'

> That is why the question of the Other, which comes back to the subject from the place from which he expects an oracular reply in some such form as *Che Vuoi*, 'what do you want?', is the one that best leads him to the path of his own desire – providing he sets out, with the help of the skills of a partner known as a psychoanalyst, to reformulate it, even without knowing it, as 'What does he want of me?' (E, p. 312).

Or as Lacan put it in another context, more clearly,

> What happens when the subject begins to speak to the analyst? – to the analyst, that is to say, to the subject who is supposed to know [i.e., the absolute Other], but of whom it is certain that he still knows nothing. It is to him that is offered something that will first, necessarily, take the form of demand. . . But what does the subject demand? That is the whole question, for the subject knows very well that, whatever his appetites may be, whatever his needs may be, none of them will find satisfaction in analysis, and that the most he can expect of it is to organize his menu (1964, p. 269).

In Lacan's view of the subject, what the subject lacks or has lost (e.g., phallus, breast, etc.) is not present in the Other; and the phenomenon of anguish makes him aware of the lack in the Other, whose 'fullness' is barred, just as it is for the subject. Thus one may write the Other as Ø, barred

Other. This has an effect on the function of the Other as the 'locus of truth' or the 'treasure of the signifier' (E, p. 316) in the signifying chain.

Lacan called S(Ø) the signifier of the barred Other or the signifier of the lack in the Other. Lack is to be seen as inherent in the very function of the Other as the 'treasure' of the signifier. The signifying chain turns around the signifier of a lack in the Other, S(Ø). Since, for Lacan, the signifier is what represents the subject for another signifier, S(Ø) is the 'signifier for which all the other signifiers represent the subject: that is to say, in the absence of this signifier, all the other signifiers represent nothing' (E, p. 316).

The introduction of the S(Ø) allows for the fact that the signifier cannot signify itself, and that there is an irreducible 'remainder' or 'leftover' in any signification. This refers to the idea that there is something basically left over, or lacking, in language, something which cannot be put into words – like Freud's kernel of our being (Kern unseres Wesens): the point, for example, where the dream reaches down into the unknown. According to Lacan, analytic experience shows that it is the property of language to slide around its own incapacity to signify an object, and the object exists then only as a *lacking object* (desire follows this movement).

This is what he called the 'objet a' (objet (a)utre, object (o)ther). It is the object which unchains desire, especially desire for what is lacking with regard to the mother, and then what the mother desires. The 'objet a' may be an orifice, a piece of breast, the anus, etc. It represents what the Other lacks in order to be absolute, represents the lack itself as the irreducible remainder in any signification. It is the object which always *escapes the subject*, and which psychoanalysis has caught in the theory of object relations, but which in Lacan's theory has a very different function. For him, this relationship turns around an edge or a cut.

The lips, the enclosure formed by the teeth, the rim of the

anus, the tip of the penis, the vagina, the slit formed by the eyelids. . . Observe that this mark of the cut is no less obviously present in the object described by analytic theory: the nipple, faeces, the phallus (imaginary object), the urinary flow. . . (A list unthinkable without adding as I do, the phoneme, the gaze, the voice, – the nothing). For is it not obvious that this feature, this partial feature, rightly emphasized in objects, is applicable not because these objects are part of a total object, the body, but because they represent only partially the function that produces them? (E✷, p. 315).

The 'objet a' is thus different from the Kleinian part object we mentioned in chapter seven, in that the 'objets a' partially represent the function which produces them, and are not parts of a total unified object. In addition,

> These objects have one common feature in my elaboration of them – they have no specular images, or in other words alterity [i.e. they are irreducible]. It is what enables them to be the 'stuffing', or rather the lining, though not in any sense the reverse of the very subject that one takes to be the subject of consciousness. For this subject, who thinks he can accede to himself by designating himself in the statement, is no more than such an object. Ask the writer about the anxiety that he experiences when faced by the blank sheet of paper, and he will tell you who *is* the turd of his phantasy (E✷, p. 315).

The 'objet a' then represents the object which is ungraspable in the mirror, the 'remainder', the lacking or lost object. The unified body image, which can be grasped in the mirror, is only the 'clothing' or the 'phantom' (semblance in French) of the lost object.

One may see how these ideas are related to the function of the Oedipus complex by returning to the role of the phallus. The lack of being of the mother is, according to Lacan, represented by the signifier of the phallus, which she does not have and which she desires. This plays an important part in determining the relations of the Oedipus complex, as Lacan understood them – how the infant identifies with the phallus, as the object lacking to, and desired by, the mother; and hence how he links himself to her lack of being through the phallus. But however strong the dual imaginary mother-child relationship is, a third term intervenes – the Other, the father. The father, as what one might call the 'Other of the m-other', brings back the mother to her own lack of a phallus, i.e., to her castration. The mother looks for what she does not have, by receiving the phallus from the father, or by identifying it with her child.

In this view of the Oedipus complex, a vicious circle is set up for the child which marks his enjoyment (jouissance). He identifies with the phallus in order to satisfy his mother's desire, and so, through the phallus, gives 'body' to his enjoyment. The phallus also signifies the law of symbolic castration for it belongs to the father, the Other who forbids the enjoyment of the mother-child 'symbiosis'. Lacan paid particular attention to the nature of this enjoyment. According to him, the subject is marked by castration from birth, as are his parents. But nevertheless, the subject's being is felt to be present, and it is linked to an 'impossible' enjoyment, impossible because of the vicious circle just described.

Lacan made an interesting distinction between jouissance (enjoyment) and plaisir (pleasure). The latter obeys Freud's principle of constancy, as described in *Beyond the Pleasure Principle*, where the psychical apparatus endeavours to keep the quantity of excitation present in it as low as possible, or at least constant. There 'exists in the mind a strong *tendency* towards the pleasure principle, but that tendency is opposed by certain other forces or circumstances, so that the final outcome cannot always be in harmony with the tendency towards pleasure' (SE 18, pp. 9-10). The ego clings to the pleasure principle, while there were also tendencies beyond the pleasure principle, 'tendencies more primitive than it and independent of it' (SE 18, p. 17), such as the repetition compulsion.

Jouissance, by contrast, goes beyond the law of constancy associated with the pleasure principle. In French jouissance includes the enjoyment of rights and property, but also the slang verb jouir, to come, and so is related to the greatest pleasure attainable, that of the sexual act. Lacan's jouissance may also be related to Freud's discharge of unbound excitatory processes, for 'unbound or primary processes give rise to far more intense feelings in both directions [pleasure and unpleasure] than the bound or secondary ones' (SE 18, p. 67).

Lacan considered that pleasure sets the limits on jouissance, 'pleasure as that which binds incoherent life together, until another, unchallengeable prohibition arises from the regulation that Freud discovered as the primary process and appropriate law of pleasure' (E, p. 319). Pleasure, for Lacan, is bound to desire as a defence against jouissance, and is a prohibition against going beyond a certain limit of jouissance. Jouissance, like death, represents *something whose limits cannot be overcome*. In Lacan's thought the 'other' of life, the negativity to be overcome, non-being (in Freudian terms the death drive) paradoxically becomes the centre of life (see below, p. 180).

If the phallic signifier has a privileged place in the unconscious, it is as a 'partial' object (not an 'objet a'), which the desired other, the mother, does not have. The phallus differs from other partial objects (breast, faeces, etc.) in being an object which she lacks and desires. It is the phallus which, according to Lacan, signifies sexual difference. It is what splits human beings into what Lacan called 'sexed partial beings'. In Aristophanes' famous myth, described in Plato's *Symposium*, each sexual half is looking desperately for the other complementary half; in Lacan's view of sexuality, the subject's search for his sexual complement is replaced by the search for that part of himself that is lost forever, owing to the fact that he or she is a sexed partial being.

In Lacan's view, the phallic signifier is a privileged signifier which structures the unconscious as a language based on a 'defect in being'. Without this defect, or the essential constituting role of lack and absence, and the lacking object, nothing could be represented. Lacan argued that the unconscious, thanks to language, can speak about the lacking object, which shines forth with its very absence. Language represents in so far as it *prohibits* – it is marked by the phallic signifier, and hence by castration, lack, absence. Thus language gives the subject the possibility of dwelling in a universe of representations and symbols; or, in Lacan's Orphic phrase, this universe is a 'defect in the purity of non-being' (E, p. 317). This seems to mean that the subject designates his being only by barring everything he signifies; and appears to be essentially how Lacan reinterpreted Freud's castration complex, and the place of death. Death becomes the origin of the subject's life – not of the imaginary life of the ego for which death merely represents a danger, but of what desire strives after. Death is the 'beyond' of desire, the forbidden, i.e., death is equivalent to enjoyment, jouissance. The unconscious strives to express what is forbidden to the speaking subject – jouissance and death.

The linguistic bar between signifier and signified now comes to take on a new meaning – the subject is barred to jouissance; desire, like language, outlines, in its movement, what is barred to the subject, and he can only express his desire for a forbidden enjoyment. Castration is basically this prohibition. The castration complex is 'the only indication of that *jouissance* which in its infinitude entails the mark of its prohibition, and which in order to constitute this mark, implies a sacrifice: that which is made in one and the same act with the choice of its symbol, the phallus' (E⋆, p. 319).

While the 'objets a' belong to the m-other (other with a little o), the mother as imaginary object, the imaginary place of enjoyment which it is impossible to symbolize, the phallus (Φ) belongs to the symbolic Other (with a capital O), and is the signifier of enjoyment.

Lacan then linked the differences between the sexes to a splitting in relation to the lack of the phallus; but not to a splitting in their being, which does not have a sex as such. He emphasized, following Freud, that there is only one libido, or sexual energy. The drives are affected by desire and are split in relation to the absence of the phallus, but the libido is a free current – it does not involve any sexual difference, and so it tends to push the drives 'adrift', as one can see in the sexual perversions. In Lacan's view of the perversions, the barred Other, Ø, is replaced by the 'objet a'. Thus the fetishist identifies the Other's lack (e.g., the castration of the woman) with an 'objet a': bits of clothing, cast-off shoes, or whatever. The hysteric identifies the demand of the Other with the Other's lack, refuses to be the object of another's desire; and is instead thrown into the realm of demands. The mother then appears as totally self-sufficient, omnipotent and hermaphroditic, while the father appears as castrated, and made unimportant in relation to the absoluteness of the mother's demands. The neurotic defends himself against desire, not wanting to accept the symbolic castration operated by the father. The neurotic's father becomes the dead father.

To summarize. We have explained the question of enjoyment as Lacan saw it; how the subject comes into being through confronting the question of his lack, and the anguish that arises when the subject is faced by the failure of the Other to live up to his or her supposed perfection. The Lacanian psycho-analytic discourse revolves around the problem of lack and of the lacking object. The subject is seen as marked by castration and lack from birth. Language represents the subject, but in so far as it represents what is prohibited. The subject is confronted by the unconscious, which is striving to express what is really forbidden to the speaking subject – jouissance and death. This inevitably creates tensions and splits in the subject, who continues to be de-centred, lacking, fading. On the one hand he tries to speak, and on the other he is faced by the impossibility of doing so. It is out of these tensions, which the subject relives in the psychoanalytic situation, that the subject comes into being.

CHAPTER TEN

ENCORE
(1972–3)

IN THE SEMINAR *Encore* Lacan tried to face the place of love in psychoanalysis. He restated some of the dilemmas that the analytic subject meets when he comes to the psychoanalyst to speak about himself, one of which is a dilemma in talking about love. Many people come to analysis precisely because they have a problem in their love relationships. But can psychoanalysis talk about love and the sexual relationship without merely moralizing? Lacan pointed out that it is, in fact, at this point that current psychoanalytic knowledge comes up against its limits, particularly when it tries to speak about feminine sexuality, about which it (like other disciplines) hardly knows what to say.

Thus *Encore* tries to deal with one of the most difficult, and yet vitally important, areas of psychoanalysis – the problem of how to talk about sexuality, and in particular feminine sexuality. One of the last important texts by Lacan, *Encore* was trying to push psychoanalysis into new territory, and it is for this reason that we end our exposition with it.

'*Encore* . . . I am always astonished that there is, without doubt, something that, as times goes on, *still* (*encore*) brings me here [or "brings me here *again*", or "*once more* brings me here" – alternative meanings of "encore"] facing you' (Lacan, 1972-3 p. 9).

With these words, Lacan opened his complicated yet

elegantly expressed twentieth seminar. His doubts about what more he had to say to his audience echo the ever-increasing demand for love made by the infant to the mother, who in turn tries to satisfy the baby's needs more and more. He thought that, as between mother and child, there was always something missing in the discourse between analyst and analysand. The analytic discourse 'turns around', 'stops and stumbles over' the same symptom – the unfulfilled and unutterable demand for love, which takes place in the analytic relationship. There is something which language cannot express, but which demands recognition; it was through this that Freud understood that what was striving to be recognized, in the painful symptoms of his hysterical patients, was related to sexuality. His patients could not talk about it; thus instead of expressing sexuality verbally they revealed the marks of sexuality on their minds and bodies.

Lacan aimed to clarify the problem of sexuality in psychoanalysis by suggesting that the object of psychoanalysis is not sexuality itself, but its effects and the problem it constitutes for the person who speaks, or the 'speaking being'. According to Lacan, psychoanalysis can do no more than describe, in its formalization, sexual intercourse as something which does not exist for the speaking being, but only exists in the silence into which the 'failing' word plunges. The analytic discourse keeps bumping into an empty space, the area excluded by language. The analyst is always faced with a resistance, the silence which represents the impossibility of knowing or speaking.

When one approaches the question of love in the psychoanalytic session the analysand often stops talking, and the analyst is faced with the realm of the inexpressible, what language is not allowed to express, except confusedly in the form of the prohibition that one must not speak about sexual intercourse. The sexual relationship involves an 'unspeakable' enjoyment, which can only be signified, as an absence, by the signifier 'love'. This signifier is the substitute for what cannot be expressed verbally about sexual intercourse.

In *Encore* Lacan discussed love in its several aspects, courtly, ecstatic and aesthetic. Much has been written about love but, according to Lacan, the many discourses of love are substitutes for something unknown about love itself, and this also applies to analysis. Thus, transference love as Lacan understood it is also marked by an absence – for instance when the patient's speech reaches a moment of resistance to the truth, which the patient formulates in terms of 'I do not want to know anything about it' (Je n'en veux rien savoir). At this point, the patient's love for the analyst can be the substitute for an experience, a 'something' which cannot be talked about, and which can mask understanding. Hopefully, the analyst does not stop at this point, and tries to analyse what appears to be inexpressible. To do so, Lacan suggested, involves the analyst in analysing his own resistance to knowing about sex, and this in turn implies questioning those psychoanalytic concepts that deal with sexuality. Here one is perhaps faced with two possibilities – either to accept that one cannot go beyond the expressible, or, as Lacan decided, to try to find new words and concepts for sexuality. One is really up against current analytic dilemmas, but, as Lacan constantly emphasized, the task of the analyst is to challenge psychoanalytic limits, which are never established once and for all. In *Encore* he hardly succeeded in answering the riddle of sex, but he did raise a number of important issues, and at the very least, he tried to point to important areas of ignorance.

The whole purpose of the seminar was to deal with what one could call the 'margins' of the analytic discourse. Indeed it seems that the analytic discourse for Lacan is always placed on the slippery edges of an abyss, which it neither ignores nor, hopefully, does it fall into it.

One might say that the experience of being led to the margins of the analytic discourse, where the ego seems to speak almost at the cost of disintegrating, is reminiscent of the subject's origins, especially when the infant is merely babbling. Lacan considered that the search for the origins of the subject, or what he ambiguously called the 'limit experience of the non-existent' (what is not created by language), had led many analysts to jump off the tracks of language. In the search for the 'pure feeling' which corresponded to the search for the thing-in-itself, they found themselves running desperately from one infantile phantom to another. In Lacan's view this desperate quest, which represented a turning away from what can be represented, could only come to a halt in front of the mysterious Real Order, the order where life meets only death and enjoyment. But the Real Order cannot be spoken about, for it does not belong to language. Even though he may speak, the subject is not allowed to know about his beginnings; he can only describe a chain of discourse around the Real which always slips away from it. All human knowledge according to Lacan is built on this 'ignorance', or what he described in partly philosophical terms as 'the original repression of the experience of not-being'.

After birth the visible world dominates, and one can say that sight guarantees the existence of things over what cannot be seen. Thus the visibility of the phallus predominates over the black hole of the female genitals. The phallus would seem to represent the knowledge of the world, and the vagina another knowledge, or rather what Lacan called a 'not-knowledge'. The phallic function includes the woman as a contingency, a part singled out within 'the gates', or 'the bars' of the feminine side, the 'dark side'. The place of the subject's origin (in the woman) is barred, or repressed. The woman functions as 'not-all' (pas toute), as a part which has to be integrated into a whole; more commonly, Lacan rightly added, this involves her in denegration or degradation. She then becomes the little other object [(a)-utre], other of being, other of the phallic function; the woman enters the Symbolic Order as a 'not-whole', a part-object serving the sub-existence of the so-called whole phallus, and thus as backing up the privileged function of the phallus in representing human identity.

Sex, however, would seem to imply a difference, a split, something missing; but also a lack of unity, and a wish to be whole. The woman – who is placed in the feminine function with only the appearance of being and of completeness, as the object which envelops an absence, the lack of the phallus – unchains the desire to be One again. But, as Lacan understood it, sexual intercourse does not work for the lovers of One, it does not work in complementarity. He considered, somewhat ambiguously, that it was rare for sexual enjoyment to be the basis of a relationship. 'We would not otherwise have so many people coming to us just to talk about this sexual relationship, which does not really exist' (Lacan, 1978, in ed. Contri, p. 211).

Referring to why, in his opinion, the sexual relationship may fail in men, Lacan wrote:

> For men, there is castration, i.e. something which negates the function of the phallus, with no hope at all of enjoying the woman's body, and of making love . . . what makes men desire, what is the cause of their desire, is cut out, restricted and logically articulated: it is this 'objet-a' which fascinates them . . . it is this 'objet-a' which allows them what Freud opposed to narcissistic love with object-love – except that what is involved is not the partner, the sexed other, but a phantom' (Lacan. 1978, in ed. Contri, p. 226).

While the man identifies with the phallus, he is bound to an enjoyment which belongs to the phallus, but, according to Lacan, at the cost of sexual enjoyment. There is something about sexual enjoyment which does not make sense, and is of no use to phallic enjoyment, which for Lacan is based on the economy of pleasure. The economy of pleasure supports all the architecture of the words and knowledge based on the 'economy' of the phallus. The phallus is the symbolic and idealized substitute for the missing sexual unity, or one-ness. Sexuality implies separation, difference and indecency (*non decet* in Latin, 'it is not proper') in relation to phallic enjoyment. Sexuality escapes from all the machinations of reason, however much reason may try to integrate it, by rationalizing, moralizing, or liberating it. Talking about love is certainly enjoyable, but at the expense of sexual enjoyment 'having its say'. The latter fails to exist for the subject who speaks, who is submitted to the symbolic structure of language. There is a 'phallic' kind of enjoyment in the symbolic operations of language which stands for, and designates at the same time, another enjoyment, connected to sexual intercourse.

The result for Lacan, in his attempt to inscribe sexuality in an analytic formalization, is that it is impossible to make sense of sexual intercourse (le rapport sexuel: sexual relationship, rapport or intercourse) at the level of language. Even the psychoanalytic experience cannot grasp the truth of sexual intercourse in its purity, and can only grasp its effects. According to Lacan sexual truth can only be looked for, in what the analysand says, as it appears and disappears in the play of his words. It is not directly expressed. We can only read the subject's desire for truth in the impossibility of his enjoying truth in language.

Phallic enjoyment is achieved in language. It is the enjoyment of mastery, of the ego's imaginary bodily compactness and mental coherence. The phallus is what everybody can see; it is the symbol of an external communal power, which forms the basis for the authority of the Symbolic Order itself, in both men and women. But, Lacan argued, if the analytic experience detected the phallic function in the economy of the subject, it was by seeing its failures, through being aware of something which says 'no' to phallic enjoyment. This can be seen in the pains of the hysteric, whose symptoms often represent a denial of the role of the phallus.

In his theory of sexuality Freud had described the libido as masculine, although his evidence for it came mainly from female hysterical patients, in which the phallic libido 'stumbled over' into the hysterical symptom in the body of the woman. Following Freud, Lacan argued that sexual difference is inscribed in language only in relation to the phallus; the *other sex* is such, only because it does not have the phallus. Woman is currently a minus, and not a whole; the woman does not make the unified One, she is the 'not-one' (pas-une) of the phallic structure of language. In this scheme, the woman comes to represent sexual difference as a remainder, a leftover, because of a split in which she cannot speak with law and authority. If she is a 'not-one', a mere vestige of something left behind by the almost-total phallus, and a little 'objet a', Lacan questioned how she can speak, and how one can speak of her. She is, and has been until now for man, an 'appearance enveloping a hole'. She has appeared to be that 'little bit more' which the phallus lacks in order to be undivided and whole. But the vagina is not a mere nothing, there is something which surrounds it – woman, who has been a mere semblance of being, yet who unchains the desire to be One again, the desire to embrace the other. The woman is the little 'objet a', the 'little thing' which makes man enjoy everything. According to Lacan, the woman's genitals cannot be truly looked at, while the shadow of the phallus plunges them into darkness. He also described how, in the case of feminine sexuality, the signifier cannot be universalized – that is, one cannot define the woman, so long as she remains in the phallic shadow, about which nothing can be said. In describing women, we have to bar the definite article, (the woman, la femme), as there is no definition of the woman which is not in the negative.

There is, as Lacan rightly pointed out, a disquieting ignorance about feminine sexuality, almost as if such ignorance were something inherent in language itself. The libido,

189

which was 'adrift' and fragmented in its origins, gets chained up, invested in and shifted from the fragmented body of the infant on to the whole 'body' of language, and on to the imaginary unity of the ego's body, which enjoys speaking. The subject gives up a fragmented sexual enjoyment by investing it in a universal symbol, the phallus. The subject cannot enjoy, in sex, being split, and the impossibility of being part of a whole being. In the sexual relationship one loves narcissistically, because love is always narcissistic in so far as it is a desire for an unreachable unity. Eros, the cohesive life energy of Freud (SE 18, pp. 50-61), tends towards One Self. The phallus offers One-ness. Psychoanalysis, according to Lacan, can question the nature of narcissism, and whether or not the subject can ever escape from it. Indeed, as he rightly pointed out, the possibility of sexual intercourse with another person (analyst, or others) is one of the most frequent topics for discussion in a psychoanalytic session.

But what, in Lacan's view, does the other want? The male's desire is particularly linked to phallic enjoyment. But what of the woman? What kind of enjoyment does she have? Lacan pointed out that we hardly know, and that psychoanalysis has barely answered these questions at all. He tried to offer some suggestions:

> if she (the woman) is excluded from the nature of things, which is the nature of words, it is just because she is not-all (pas-toute), she has, in relation to what the phallic function designates as enjoyment, a supplementary enjoyment. Notice I said *supplementary*. If I had said *complementary*, where would it lead us? We would fall into the 'whole' (1972-3, p. 68).

Thus Lacan explains the woman's enjoyment as having something extra, supplementary, 'encore!'. She has a surplus of enjoyment which cannot be integrated into language, unless it is placed under a prohibition, such as the law of castration. Might the woman, who after all does not risk much when faced by the threat of castration (only men have something that can be castrated), be partly exempt from the pursuance of this law? The woman might know something about sexual enjoyment, though she does not confess to it. The surplus of enjoyment left over by language becomes the unconfessable crime which is pursued by the law of the father, who is the upholder of the phallus as legislative power. The law looks for the truth, but only to put it behind bars, to keep truth on the run, from one signifier to another; the truth retreats and re-appears like a mirror-image, a *semblant*, it moves in and out like waves lapping on the shore, still it goes on, encore . . . disguised, mute, fading away, ungraspable.

Lacan had the interesting thought that the woman experiences an enjoyment which she does not even know about.

> There is an enjoyment which belongs to her, to this *her* (*elle*) which does not exist and does not mean anything. There is an enjoyment which belongs to her and about which she does not know anything, apart from her experiencing it – this she does know. She obviously knows about it when it happens to her. It does not happen to all women (1972-3, p. 69).

It is as if, Lacan speculated, the woman, in her role of 'not-being', in the safety of the dark side in which she is placed, might come into contact with death, the disturbing truth which 'enlightened' knowledge has to renounce in order to exist. Pleasure is what delimits the subject's encounter with death; pleasure also leaves behind, as a surplus, the remains of enjoyment, which do not serve what Lacan called the 'master-being' (m'être, a play on words from maître, master, and être, to be or being), the enjoyment of mastery and being, involved in phallic enjoyment. This surplus of enjoyment is a surplus because it does not even serve biological survival. In the unknown enjoyment of the woman there must be an unknown truth, which resembles the mystical experience of ecstasy – as if the woman, in going beyond phallic enjoyment and not being totally submitted to its limitations, acquires something *more* which, as with the mystics, puts her in touch with God. Lacan speculated that maybe the woman, while leaving the phallus to man, might actually have contact with it. The man *is* the phallus, he enjoys 'being' the phallus, but the woman may be the one who can really have contact with it.

This enjoyment of the woman can be compared to the culminating moment of a relationship with God. It involves an unknown knowledge, in so far as it does not belong to the human sphere but to divine knowledge, which, in ecstasy, appears to overlap with divine enjoyment. 'It is as it was for St. Theresa – you have only to go to Rome and see Bernini's statue, to understand at once that she is, without doubt, in the act of enjoying. And what does she enjoy? It is clear that the essential testimony of mystics consists in saying that they experience it, but do not know anything about it' (1972-3, p. 71).

In spite of their increased consciousness of the limits that their role imposes on their human identity, women seem to be caught up in their own elusiveness. As Freud himself wrote: 'Throughout history people have knocked their heads against the riddle of the nature of femininity. . . Nor will you have escaped worrying over this problem – those of you who are men; to those of you who are women this will not apply – you yourselves are this problem' (SE 22, p. 113). Lacan said, 'We have implored our women psychoanalysts, on our bended knees, to tell us about it [the enjoyment of the woman], but mum's the word!' (1972-3, p. 69).

One might say that the 'hegemony' of the phallus in language is such that, in the power of its discourse and discipline, psychoanalysis itself has tended to give up contemplating any disturbing or subverting effect that a woman might reveal in her enjoyment. Even Freud, as a man, could only follow his women patients with phallic parameters. His understanding could not go beyond the revelation that something 'hurts' and 'pains' beyond the phallus, that something is there beyond the phallus and speaks in the body of the woman, something that says 'no' to phallic enjoyment. Lacan's substantial achievement in this field was that he opened up the nature of feminine enjoyment for analytic research. What does the woman want? Does she want to keep her enjoyment to herself, in the silence of her submission? Or does she strive for words to speak about it, and if so, does she run the risk of losing it? From where does this submission of woman to man come from? Is it submission or complicity? These were Lacan's questions.

In *The Second Sex* Simone de Beauvoir points out how the woman can easily fall into the existential temptation of running away from her own freedom in order to avoid 'the anguish and tension of an authentically assumed existence'. According to de Beauvoir, the woman is complacent in her role of other, of being an object, alienated in the passivity proper to the symbolic category of the feminine. Up to now, woman has enjoyed the phallus only at the price of playing the role of the one who is castrated, and debarring herself from a whole subjectivity. 'She is merely what man has decided for her . . . she appears to man as an essentially sexed being. . . She is determined and differentiated in relation to man and not to herself: she is the inessentiality, he is the Absolute, she is the Other' (de Beauvoir, p. 16).

Lacan added that the problem of women's alienation is that she happens to love. She is within the order of the phallus, because she, like man, loves to be One. Like her partner, she believes in the 'soul', and she wants to enjoy it. However much she is pushed back into her shelter of joyful not-being, she also enjoys being.

Lacan pointed out that in psychoanalytic theories the woman comes out of her encounter with the phallus, and consequently with the law of the father, as castrated. But

193

castrated of what? Not of the phallus, because she does not have one, but of her own sexuality. Lacan pointed out that it is often thought to be 'decent' and 'sightly' for the woman to keep her genitals hidden, and not to disturb man's ignorance about the realm of the uncastrated feminine world. There is also a tendency to appreciate only her superficial form. The 'beauty' of her body is the veil covering her genitals. The round, worshipped maternal body hides the disturbing darkness of the subject's origins and the wound that both penetration and birth leave behind on the 'virgin-whole-body' of the woman. The woman does not come out unscathed from her encounter with the phallus (however pleasurable this may be) as it takes possession of her body in order to deflorate and impregnate her. The baby, 'torn' away from her body, is the substitute for the woman's phallus, and is symbolically restored to the father, who gives his name and identity to it. The symbolic place of the mother, like the place of origin, is empty. The mother, the forbidden object of enjoyment, both for the boy and the girl, remains a myth, or a gynaecological product.

One could say that, apart from an ideal respect for the sacrifices involved in maternity, the mother's attempts to intervene with her product are tolerated as the enigma that man has to allow to his producer. Many women analysts today, in the attempt to find a specific feminine ground of investigation, are looking at the experience of maternity as an enjoyment which belongs to the woman only at the real and imaginary levels. But one could say that her deprivation takes place at the symbolic level, where in Lacanian terms she is the loser by definition.

One could also say that the recent rapid changes in the human and social status of the woman have led to a crisis in the attempt to make the difference between the sexes a mere question of complementarity. Men and women cannot merely be seen as two sides of the same being, but as two different beings. The feminist movement has been reclaiming and re-evaluing feminine status, on the two axes of the phallus and the other. This has included a re-evaluation of sexual difference, either as being an unimportant biological contingency or as entailing a re-evaluation of the feminine as such, with attempts to express, release, and reveal it. But how, Lacan asked, can the woman express herself in language without subverting her very essence, which is to disown (méconnaitre) the indecent truth of her enjoyment?

In *Encore* Lacan tried to meet women at this crossroads in the problem of their identity, an identity difficult to disentangle from the role women have had for centuries. *Encore* continues to be the subject of intense interest among psychoanalysts on the Continent, and also among feminists, both there and in England. Although hardly solving all the mysteries of feminine sexuality, Lacan opened up a series of important issues. He tried to face the dilemma of woman's enjoyment, to what extent this enjoyment goes beyond the ordinary phallic parameters, and how far our language has been unnecessarily confined to phallic parameters. Finally he implied that our understanding of both the Oedipus complex and of sexuality needs a revision which takes account of feminine enjoyment.

CHAPTER ELEVEN

SUMMARY AND RECENT DEVELOPMENTS

LACAN'S main intention as a writer and an analyst was to restore psychoanalysis to life by a radical return to the writings of Freud and by putting psychoanalysis in touch with the latest developments in contemporary thought. He constantly emphasized what was radical, revolutionary and difficult to accept in psychoanalysis, and castigated those who tried to make Freud's insights into the basis of a model of social adjustment, and adaptation to so-called reality. In Lacan's opinion, the task of psychoanalysis was to *question* the nature of this reality, not to feel comfortable with it.

As an analyst Lacan made five important contributions which we have examined in detail in the text: a revision of our understanding of Freud's texts; a revision of Freudian theory on the basis of linguistic concepts; a constant, fruitful challenging of the limits of psychoanalysis; a serious attempt to examine the status of analytic knowledge in the light of new areas of thought in other disciplines; and an unorthodox approach to analytic training.

It is not as easy to summarize his contributions as a general thinker and the impact of his ideas outside psychoanalysis. But Lacan was, and remains, widely influential for a variety of reasons. First of all, he was a part of French culture, where there is less separation of different disciplines than in many countries, and where it is easy for specialists from different disciplines to exchange ideas. But perhaps more importantly, as Bowie (1979, p. 151) has described, 'his writing proposes itself consciously as a critique of all discourses and all ideologies'. Lacan seemed to reveal the subversive actions of the unconscious in a wide variety of disciplines or 'discourse and ideologies'. Practitioners of other disciplines, who have also wished to evolve a non-reductive approach to their work, have used Lacan's discoveries. In England, for example, the influence of Lacanian ideas has been until recently mainly confined to cinema criticism, feminism, literary criticism, and some areas of marxism. Interesting though some of these influences may be, the Lacanian ideas often seem to be cut off from their *essential* roots in clinical psychoanalysis. In Paris, on the other hand, the influence of Lacan is not only felt in many areas of thought, but still involves the active participation of psychoanalysts.

Lacan was a formidable man. He was a serious thinker, who inspired intense loyalty but also great hate; he was perhaps an important writer, he certainly created a unique psychoanalytic style; and he has had a great influence on French, and now increasingly, international culture. He was rarely a 'good advert' for the seriousness of analytic practice, being very flamboyant, and often taking great pains to make fun of the official psychoanalytic movement, or of any institution. Indeed, once his own school of psychoanalysis was firmly established, and looked at last as if it were an institution, he dissolved it, apparently with few regrets. But in the end, he will have to be judged on his work. Such a judgement is a hard task, because of his style, and because of the density of his thought. It is also perhaps too soon to make a thorough assessment of his work.

We have tried to explain his main concepts as clearly as possible, and we have included a limited amount of critical appraisal. This has often entailed interpreting his ambiguous prose, and perhaps reducing much of its power and fascination, and its play with signifiers. This was obviously necessary in such a work, but it does mean that the almost poetical quality of much of his writing has been diminished in the process of presentation. Although one can justifiably take issue with this poetical quality, as at times Lacan's poetry seems to interfere with the argument of his thought, it also gives him a unique voice.

If psychoanalysis were strictly a natural science, then one would require an analytic author to explain himself in sober explanatory prose. However, the status of psychoanalysis is ambiguous. It is a therapy for people with problems, yet it is also a method for exploring and understanding the psyche (or, as Lacan once put it, a 'conjectural science of the human subject'), and these two elements often seem to be incompatible. Ideally, there should be some kind of unity of theory and practice, but this is rare. Lacan's point of view, which is very useful, is that language is what is common to both theory and practice, for psychoanalysis is the 'talking cure'. In his view, this simple yet revolutionary discovery of Freud's had been forgotten, and Lacan considered that it was his task to restore psychoanalysis to its proper field of study – 'The function and field of speech and language'. He considered, with some justification, that the attempt to look beyond language for the subject's truth, or the attempt to make psychoanalysis into a sub-speciality of a scientific psychology, was a fundamental méconnaissance of Freud's discoveries.

We suggested in the Introduction that differences in attitudes to Lacan on the Continent and in England and America reflected fundamental cultural differences. It is of some use to spell out some of these differences in more detail, and to examine Lacan's place in his intellectual and cultural milieu. The way that Lacan thought, argued and, above all, the way that he used language make him obviously French, and the French have always been proud of their means of expression. Theodore Zeldin (1980) has shown how the secondary school system, from the nineteenth century onwards, instilled and defended certain qualities of thought that made the Frenchman unique, and which one can certainly detect in Lacan's work.

French schools distinguished themselves from most of Europe by teaching philosophy to children, indeed the senior forms in the secondary schools were called 'classes de philosophie'. Thus, as Zeldin has pointed out, the élite of the nation were provided with a very particular intellectual training, in marked contrast to that provided for the English. It was in these classes that 'Frenchmen learned their characteristic abstract . . . vocabulary, their skill in classification and synthesis, in solving problems by rearranging them verbally, their rationalism and scepticism . . . and their ability to argue elegantly and apparently endlessly' (p. 207).

What was supposed to distinguish French philosophy from that of other countries was that it tried not to be a technical speciality, but a general survey of the whole of life. It sought to stimulate reflection rather than inculcate knowledge. The philosophy teacher, and the philosophy class, in which the teacher set an example by giving a personal lecture, expressing his own opinions while giving due consideration to those of others, became the model for intellectual life. The teachers formed pressure groups which spread their influence beyond the intellectual élite. A typical example is that of Sartre who, with several other philosophy teachers, formed the journal *Les Temps Modernes* in 1945. More recently, the explosion of the power, vigour and influence of French philosophy can be seen as an extension and development of forces in the means of education that can be traced back to the nineteenth century.

Innovating as French philosophy has become since the 1940s, a more conservative thread has also influenced it. This thread, of which the work of the philosopher Alain is a typical example, rejected originality as neither desirable nor possible, instead considering that philosophy was not a system but a style. To a great extent philosophy then became a literary exercise, in which 'the studied expression of obvious ideas in impressive language took precedence over the solution of problems' (p. 214). In addition, the rhetoric class became popular from the late nineteenth century. There was taught the 'discours' – the art of making speeches, writing letters and self-expression, in such a way as to show one's taste and education, rather similar to the classical English education, and based on the models of ancient Greece and Rome.

This general prestige of philosophy helped to stimulate the introduction of new ideas into France, particularly from Germany. Though rhetoric might be superficial as a self-contained study, it helped to create enthusiasm.

> French ideas were often presented in a way that gave the impression that new continents were being discovered, or rather were about to be discovered. The excitement generated made intellectual life probably more exhilarating than anywhere else in the world, even if the excitement had to be paid for with the subsequent gloom of disappointment (p. 242).

The May 1968 revolution was in part an attempt to revitalize the French education system, which in many ways had become stultified and conservative, even though the general cultural life of Paris had continued to be invigorating.

One can see in Lacan's thought many uniquely French influences in his emphasis on style, his intellectualist approach, his passion for words, and his respect for philosophy. The very fact that he was able to form his Seminar, and that it became a focus for the dissemination of his ideas, and provided the audience with a particular 'discours', cannot be isolated from the importance already given in France to the philosophy class and the role of the personal lecture. However, enmeshed in the French tradition as he was, Lacan was also fighting to subvert its very foundations.

In this sense one can see him as very much part of the revolutionary and subversive thread in French culture as well as a follower of the radical current in psychoanalysis.

Of course, one important problem when exploring the relationship between psychoanalysis and other disciplines, and hence the place of psychoanalysis in culture, is the status of psychoanalysis itself. As we have often mentioned, there has been considerable disagreement about how much it is a natural science, how much an art, or how much it is, as Lacan in general considered, one of the human sciences and as such concerned with the nature of meaning. Some analysts, such as the American ego psychologists, consider that psychoanalytic propositions fulfil the general requirements of theory in science; that is, that psychoanalysis refers to a complex set of constructs and general assumptions on which specific hypotheses are based, and to a broad framework for the study of human behaviour, which allows for the study of a large number of independent factors. They consider that one has to take advantage of the differentiated tools that analytic theory offers as a critical method for conceptualizing human behaviour, when considering the contribution of psychoanalysis to other fields of study. In essence this represents the 'positivist' approach to the nature of science and is reflected in the work of Karl Popper, who provided clear boundaries for the status of a science – the falsifiability of hypotheses. There used to be considerable controversy about whether or not psychoanalysis could be considered in any way a science along Popperian lines. Indeed, it would certainly be very difficult to formulate falsifiable hypotheses in the manner of Popper while treating a patient in the consulting room. But the explosion of interest in the human sciences does provide an alternative method of interpreting psychoanalytic phenomena to that proposed by positivism. For example, the German philosopher Habermas (1978) has succinctly delineated the status of psychoanalysis. He considers that it is a science of man, not a natural science, and that what is unique to it is its discovery of a particular kind of 'self-reflection'. It is through this that the human subject can free himself from states in which he may become an 'object' for himself, i.e., a 'thing', a mere object of scientific curiosity, or a commodity. The specific activity of self-reflection must be accomplished by the subject himself.

Lacan would probably have broadly agreed with this formulation. He also once suggested that psychoanalysis be considered as an art in a special sense – one of the classical 'liberal arts', which included astronomy, music, dialectics, arithmetic and grammar. These liberal arts were distinguished by the importance they attached to what one could call a fundamental relation to human proportion. Seen in this light, psychoanalysis does seem to preserve something of such a proportional relation of man to himself.

Lastly, although it is clear that Lacan viewed psychoanalysis as a human science, involved with questioning the nature of the human subject, there remains some ambiguity about how he thought he related to contemporary thinkers outside psychoanalysis. There are references, particularly in the fifties, to the anthropologist Lévi-Strauss, the philosopher Hyppolite, and the work of linguists such as Jakobson, but Lacan always seemed to maintain an independent attitude. It is partly for this reason that it is difficult to understand in detail the nature of his relations with thinkers outside psychoanalysis. Yet, as we have often emphasized, he was first and foremost a psychoanalyst, and although one may try to place him in a uniquely French context, he remained part of the international analytic movement, which goes beyond individual cultures. Thus, one may see Lacan as uniquely French, with French preoccupations and influences, in debt to philosophy and structural linguistics, and partly influenced by his contemporaries outside the field of psychoanalysis. But he still saw his own place in the twentieth century as that of a revitalizer and reinterpreter of

Freud, a psychoanalyst talking to psychoanalysts.

We have so far limited our account to following the 'flow' of Lacan's thought, and have kept in the background the impact of his thought and personality on psychoanalysis. We will now attempt to redress the balance, and also to summarize some of the recent developments in Lacanian psychoanalysis.

Psychoanalysis, like other branches of knowledge, has felt the influence of a small number of important thinkers who have determined its major trends of research and development. The difference between psychoanalysis and other branches of knowledge, however, is that there is relatively little academic transmission of its knowledge. Indeed, one could say that Lacan had his toughest battles around the whole issue of the transmission of psychoanalysis to other analysts.

One also observes that analysts remain too tied to the personal authority of the few major thinkers. Freud himself had a strong sense of personal ownership of his discoveries, although the way that he felt towards his 'child' changed over the years. In the early years, for example, he considered that a psychoanalyst was any individual who practised analysis, read and commented on his work, and made theoretical contributions to the new discipline. In short, transmission of psychoanalysis was informal, and almost a 'family business'.

With the founding of the International Psychoanalytic Association (IPA) in 1910 came a move to extend Freud's teaching more adequately, and in an international context. At the 1910 Nuremberg Congress Freud maintained that a self-analysis was indispensable for the practice of analysis; but he did not clarify whether or not he meant an analysis conducted by another person. The Zurich school, led by Jung, recommended that anyone who wished to carry out analyses on other people should first undergo an analysis by someone with expert knowledge. But it was only in 1922, at the International Congress of the IPA in Berlin (and in Freud's absence), that it was stipulated that a training analysis was obligatory for any would-be analyst. This new rule inaugurated a proper training for analysts, controlled by an institution and with certain regulations.

Once the body of his doctrines was established, and its acceptance fairly widespread, Freud himself became somewhat preoccupied with a fear of losing control over his discoveries – either because of an excess of passive dependency on the part of his followers, together with their narrow-minded attitude of obedience; or because of deviations in theory and practice on the part of his best and most creative pupils, specifically Jung, Adler and Rank. Given these two attitudes to his work, neither of them satisfactory, the aging Freud found himself having to give in to the institutionalization of psychoanalysis, hoping that this would guarantee the continuity of his thought. But the institutionalization of Freud's thought has led to a number of conflicts and tensions within psychoanalysis, and has often led to a stultification of thought.

Such conflicts, the direct result of Freud's difficulty in dealing with his new discovery, exploded like a whirlwind with Lacan. It is difficult to know whether or not Lacan played on the essential paradoxes of the institutional framework of analysis, or was a victim of the institution's machinations. He himself claimed that he did not wish to be expelled from the IPA, nor did he want to become a hero, and that he was forced to continue his teaching as best he could. Indeed, the IPA's treatment of Lacan was typical of their attitude. They reacted to the threat that Lacan represented with an astonishing degree of paranoia – astonishing only because psychoanalysts are supposed to be relatively free of such an attitude – and with little serious discussion of his ideas. Instead they seem to have made judgements based on hearsay and gossip.

Such an approach to Lacan in fact merely increased his influence, without the IPA being able to have any control over him, or any capacity to act as 'diplomats' in disputes over his ideas. With hindsight, the IPA would probably have been wiser had they attempted to keep Lacan within the fold, and thus keep the whirlwind at bay. However, it is also clear that by the sixties, Lacan was able to maintain his school quite happily without interference from the IPA. His seminar became a popular topic of conversation among the intelligentsia, while his texts were enthusiastically circulated under the counter among the student population. He stirred up considerable interest in Freud and psychoanalysis, and became a sort of cult hero, apparently much to his disgust. What stirred everyone up was that he seemed to be challenging the basis of French academic education, and to be offering some sort of 'forbidden fruit' to those hungry for new ideas. It was thus not surprising that Lacan became linked to the student explosion of 1968.

Catherine Clément (1981) has described vividly the excitement of those days. She points out how Lacan could be thought-provoking and exhilarating in the flesh; she retained a basic core of genuine admiration and worthwhile experience, and is thankful for having been exposed to the 'myth' of the Seminar. Her account shows clearly the kind of transference love that was stirred up in the seminars, and got out of hand. This was much to Lacan's surprise, although he of course must also be held responsible for the consequences. Clément describes how it was her own daughter who pointed out to her, innocently, that she was obviously in love with Lacan.

> Yes, I loved him, and like most of my generation I was in love with thought – this fascination with thought irritates those who do not participate in it. When you are always on time for an appointment and nothing can make you miss it, when you leave disappointed but charmed, what

else is it but love? Oh, I know that all this does not sound respectable today. . . True, we call it dogmatism, and [say] that this sort of love produces self-betrayal, rigidity and thoughtlessness. Yet, another sort of thought may arise in the same process – which fights against itself and which finally destroys its object. It keeps a 'basic core' attached to the loved object, and retains what had aroused the love at the beginning of the process (p. 23).

One may then understand the attachment shown to Lacan as a transferential process, involving a sort of love which, as Freud claimed, is just as true as other kinds of love. Transference is unavoidable in analytic work, but needs to be overcome at the end of that work. One could say that the end of an analysis, or of an analyst's formation, occurs when he has stopped loving or hating his analyst and his analytic masters.

Clément also says that the greatest dilemma for those who followed Lacan has been how to cope with his death. There was a considerable amount of frenzied agitation around him just before his death, with people hanging on to his every word as if it were to be his last, and as if each sentence were full of absolute wisdom. Lacan himself attempted to throw off such conservative adoration by liquidating his own school – an act supposedly aimed not against those who loved him, but against those who loved him too much, as well as those who came to hate him. Indeed, many Lacanian analysts today describe the events that led to the dissolution of the Ecole Freudienne as a 'civil war' between love and hate.

Many crucial arguments before and after Lacan's death about the future of Lacanianism were centred on the procedure of the 'pass' (La Passe). The pass constituted the passage from the title of ordinary member of the school to analyst of the school. It was the only part of the Ecole that was official, as all other activities were based on individual choice and responsibility – even the decision to practise analysis was based on self-authorization, that is, the individual could authorize himself to practise as an analyst. In fact even the pass itself was a voluntary undertaking. The candidate chose a number of people (the 'passers') to represent him at a committee which was elected from the membership of the school. The candidate himself never went before the committee. As Schneiderman (1983, p. 80) has written,

> Because the passers go before the committee in place of the candidate, the personal presence of the candidate ought not to exert undue influence on the committee's deliberations. The candidate for the pass has been called upon to show that he can speak through others, from another place. This is not the same as to say that the candidate will make his passers into his mouthpieces, simply expressing what he would have said were he there in person. The passers are not there to tell the candidate's story. What they will tell is the effect of his story on them. And the committee will judge whether this candidate is an Orlando still pining for the love of his Rosalind, whether he is a Lear railing against the universe and his ungrateful daughters, or whether he has reached the state I have identified with Prospero. This last state means that he has renounced his narcissism, both the pathological and the normal varieties, that he fully accepts the split between his act of speaking and what is heard of what he has said, that he accepts being in the position of the dead only after his discourse has earned him that position. At this point he will have passed the pass.

There arose various factions within the school, each of them having different attitudes to the pass, and varying degrees of faithfulness to Lacan. There were those who were totally opposed to the procedure of the pass, and those who disagreed on certain details of the procedure. Some thought it

THE WORKS OF JACQUES LACAN

could not be an appropriate guarantee of the candidate's capacity to become an analyst, and some that it was true to the spirit of Lacanianism. Lacan himself seems to have taken a somewhat ambiguous and distant attitude to what was going on around him. But as matters got out of hand, with people at each other's throats, he intervened by liquidating the school. This act was interpreted by followers as a political act and by opponents as authoritarian, although it was quite consistent with his whole attitude to his school and to psychoanalysis. It was very much like the way he would suddenly bring a session to an end, unexpectedly breaking off the analysand's discourse, apparently as a way of telling the analysand not to be too fascinated with what he had to say. Schneiderman describes what it felt like to be at the receiving end of Lacan's short sessions, and their meaning for him. 'The ending of the session, unexpected and unwanted, was like a rude awakening, like being torn out of a dream by a loud alarm. . . The gesture of breaking the session, of cutting it off, was a way of telling people to put things to the side, to move forward, not to get stuck or fascinated by the aesthetics of the dream' (1983, pp. 132 ff).

One can argue that the whole idea of the short session is disturbing, and counter to much of the analytic process, particularly if one has been trained in the British tradition, which emphasizes the holding environment, the role of early mothering and the need for the analyst to be consistent. Lacan's tradition, however, was more that of the 'father'. One could say he emphasized the need for the analyst, like a forbidding father, to represent, and point out to the analysand, the Other. He was expelled from the IPA ostensibly because of it, and because of its effects on his analytic candidates. However, one may note that he was using the short session, with official knowledge and approval, long before the French analytic society split into different factions.

For Lacan dissolution of his school meant that the

moment had come for his pupils to separate from him, whether they wanted to or not. His seminars and school were probably his short sessions for the group of analysts, broken off at the moment he considered it ripe to achieve a meaningful effect, somewhat regardless of what the group wished. As he wrote at the time, 'If I per(e)severe (père, father) it is because I am relying on a counter-experience to compensate for the previous experience. I do not need a lot of people, and there are people I do not really need. I leave them in the lurch so that they can show me what they can do' (Lacan, 1982, p. 15).

Like an analysand who has not come to the termination of his analysis, a number of people did not consider that their formation was terminated, that is, they did not feel that they had 'passed'. Traditional analytic training evokes and uses the power of the transference, often without its being recognized or dispelled as such, to foster a certain amount of infantile dependency on the part of its members on those in authority, who give the comforts of professional respectability in exchange. All of Lacan's actions were instead aimed at dispelling the power of the transference at work in the transmission of psychoanalysis.

One can also imagine that Lacan wished to be killed, like the father of the 'primal horde' described by Freud in *Totem and Taboo*, in order to make his teaching active, meaningful and challenging. Indeed, the passions of love and hate unleashed in his followers vividly remind one of Freud's myth of the primal father, with his absolute and arbitrary law, which made him possessor of all power, chattels and women; a man whose sons desired only his death, that they might be free. But an identification with the figure of the absolute father, however loved and loving one wants him to be, only serves the neurotic, and the analytic candidate alike, as a means of hiding their own truth. Such an identification with the Other can itself lead to passive dependency, and to the alienation of the subject's truth, and is very different from a true encounter with the Other, the ultimate aim of a Lacanian analysis.

In Lacanian terms, one could say that the subject's truth consists in his own deficiency and lack. The subject clings to the law of the father, in order to deny and ward off his encounter with the fragmentary and often incomprehensible laws of the world, and to defer his encounter with the ultimate 'masters' of sexual enjoyment and death. Thus, the analyst can never gratify the function of always knowing the subject's truth, which the analysand asks of him. Although the analyst is the one who is 'supposed to know' the truth, he really has to give up the power associated with his position in order to encourage the encounter with the Other. The analyst, according to Lacan, should not identify with the Other, but only encourage the analysand to encounter his own Other. The analyst has to help the analysand 'unstick' himself from the wish that the analyst knows the truth. Lacan also claimed that it was in order to 'unstick' those who were attached by too much 'glue' to his school, and to his authority, that he formed the Cause Freudienne 'at a stroke'. In fact the result was that after his death, many Lacanians felt not only unstuck but lost. It was as if Lacan had wished the whirlwind to strike, leaving behind bits of debris strewn around. It will no doubt take some time to see how all the debris – the scattered bits of the Lacanian movement – will settle, if at all.

The aim of the Cause Freudienne is illustrated in Article Two of its statutes, drawn up by Lacan (Lacan, 1982, p. 81). 'This Association has psychoanalysis as its object. And its aim is to reinstate its truth, transmit its knowledge, and to offer it to scientific control and debate, and consequently to found the qualification of the psychoanalyst. Its aim is to orientate those who wish to carry on with Lacan the field opened up by Freud.' After Lacan's death in 1981 his son-in-law, Jacques-Alain Miller, whom Lacan had chosen as his heir, became director of the Cause. Over a period of time, however, several important figures resigned from the new school. These analysts included Françoise Dolto, Michèle Montrelay, Moustapha Safouan, Serge Leclaire, and Octave and Maud Mannoni.

The Cause and its members are considered by other-groups as having misused Lacan's name. These groups reacted to the dissolution, which they considered an authoritarian act, by forming their own organizations. What distinguishes the Cause is an academic emphasis on the interpretation of Lacan's work and of his mathematical formulation, the 'mathemes'. This gave rise to considerable criticism from some of the other groups, who took up the Lacanian emphasis on inventiveness and the independence of the individual analyst's work and thought. Nevertheless the Cause has maintained a teaching organization, with work and study groups called 'cartels', meetings called 'forums', conferences, library facilities and numerous weekly and monthly publications. In order to be a member, one has only to be part of a 'cartel', a small study group composed of four people, plus a fifth person who acts as 'witness', invigilating and elaborating on the effects of the group's work. Such a group can run for only two years, in order, they claim, to prevent too many 'gluing' effects. The many magazines attached to the Cause include *L'Ane*, *Ornicar*, *Analytica*, *L'Acropole* and *Les Bloc-notes*.

Some of the analysts who signed a statement (réfère) against the dissolution formed a provisional group called 'Entre-temps' (in between times) to give themselves time, as it were, to overcome the shock of what had happened, and to sort out their position. After three years of provisional status, they finally constituted what they call their own 'space'. Instead of cartels, they have 'ateliers' and 'collectives', study groups where one's own participation does not need to be declared. Their conferences and meetings are called 'psychoanalytic events', and their main publication is called *L'Espace* (Space). They are characterized by their willingness to exchange ideas with other groups and institutions, including foreign ones; their notion that the 'space' offers a certain amount of 'distance' from struggles and splits; and a tendency to play down the idealization of Lacan and the central role of the signifier in analytic theory.

Some analysts who had at first adhered to the Cause later opposed its statutes, which they considered both sectarian and contrary to the formation of an analyst. An alternative institutional framework was attempted in March 1981 with the setting up of the 'Centre d'Etudes et de Recherches Freudienne' (Centre for Freudian Study and Research) by Charles Melman, Jean Clavreul and Solange Falade. But this centre had a short life because of disagreements amongst its founders, who later formed other groups.

Octave and Maud Mannoni, who refused to maintain the pass, founded their own 'Centre de Formation et de Recherches Psychanalytiques' (Centre of Psychoanalytic Formation and Research) in 1982. It still continues to do interesting clinical work and research, in conjunction with specialists of various other disciplines. 'Confrontation', led by René Major, and 'Le Collège de Psychanalyse' only organize congresses and meetings which all the schools can attend. They do not wish to form an institution, rather to promote information and research. In 1983 the group 'Cartels Constituants de l'Analyse Freudienne' (Component Groups of Freudian Analysis) was formed. As with most of the other post-Lacanian groups, the discussion of the emblematic issue of the pass and its function in relation to the self-authorization of the analyst is one of its central preoccupations. Lastly, a group of the 'solitaires' (those analysts who have remained somewhat independent of the other groups) formed 'La Convention Analytique' (Analytic Convention) in 1983, and has recently included Moustapha Safouan, who continues to convene his important seminars. Serge Leclaire has chosen to remain working in isolation.

Having sketched the fragmented scene of the Lacanian movement, it would be unfair to look down at it with the superior attitude of those who think they can do without a similar 'whirlwind'. Although there is apparent unity in the British Psycho-Analytical Society, the unity is based on a tendency to exclude itself from external influences, for instance from cross-fertilization from other disciplines. Although such an attitude is rather British, there are signs, as in France, of an increase of interest in psychoanalysis outside the official institutions. In addition, there is widespread interest in Lacanianism in various parts of the world, especially in South America, which has so far resulted in bitter and anxious disputes between official and unofficial psychoanalytic organizations. It rather looks as if psychoanalysis itself, as a field of knowledge, has to go through the same, unavoidable process as a personal analysis, that is, the process peculiar to the analytic search for truth, with a series of stages of splitting and disavowal before the truth is clarified. However bitter it may feel, psychoanalysis may be going through a process similar to the final stage of an analysis, when the last phantoms of the ego break into pieces. British psychoanalysis may still be just holding on to the illusory unity of its 'ego'. But if psychoanalysis has to deal with its own phantoms and symptoms, there exists no 'super-analyst' to analyse them. Perhaps the message that Lacan has transmitted is that analysts have to deal with the symptoms themselves.

ADDENDA

APPENDIX 1

SCHEMATIC OUTLINE OF SOME RELEVANT LINGUISTIC CONCEPTS

O NE CAN SEE linguistics as a part of the general study of the science of signs, or Semiology. The question of the sign was taken up many times by ancient, medieval and Renaissance thinkers, but it was Locke, in his division of the three branches of knowledge who coined the term Semeiotica for the doctrine of signs, 'the most usual whereof being words, as to communicate our thoughts to one another, as well as to record them for our own use, signs of our ideas are also necessary: those which men have found most convenient, and therefore generally make use of, are articulate sounds' (Locke, Book 4, chapter 20). Saussure also conceived of a 'science that studies the life of signs within society' which he called Semiology, (Saussure, p. 16), which included symbolic rites, military signals, polite formulae, etc., with language being the most important system. We will confine this outline to linguistics.

Faced with the 'confused mass of heterogenous and unrelated things' which make up language, Saussure divided language (le langage) into two dialectically related aspects – la langue and la parole. Because in English there is no word that distinguishes between langage and langue, we will call the former language, and keep to the French for the latter; we translate parole as speech.

La langue is the language system, which for Saussure was the true and unique object of linguistic study.

La langue is a well-defined object in the heterogenous mass of language facts. It can be localized in the limited segment of the speaking-circuit where an auditory image becomes associated with a concept. It is the social side of language, outside the individual who can never create nor modify it by himself. . . La langue is homogeneous. It is a system of signs in which the only essential thing is the union of meanings and sound-images, and in which both parts of the sign are psychological (Saussure, p. 15).

Thus la langue is a social object, the social part of language, a systematized set of rules and conventions, a code. It is a 'storehouse filled by the members of a given community through their active use of speech, a grammatical system that has a potential existence in the mind of each speaker or more specifically in the minds of groups of individuals' (Saussure, p. 13).

Speech is the executive side of language. It is an individual act, the message. Within the speech act, there can be distinguished the combinations by which the speaker uses the code of la langue to express thoughts, and the psycho-physical mechanism that allows him to do so.

In separating la langue from speech, 'we are at the same time separating: (1) what is social from what is individual; and (2) what is essential from what is accessory and more or less accidental' (Saussure, p. 14).

But each of these terms is dependent on the other – there is no langue without speech, and no speech without la langue. Nothing enters la langue without starting in speech, and no speech is possible if it is not drawn from la langue.

Given that la langue is a system of signs, we will now outline Saussure's concepts of the linguistic sign, and of how signs are linked.

For Saussure, the linguistic sign (signe) is a double entity, made up of a concept (the signified, signifié) with a sound-image (the signifier, signifiant). The act which binds signifier and signified is signification. The sound-image is not a material sound, a purely physical thing, but the psychological imprint of the sound, the impression it makes on the senses. Thus the Latin word 'arbor' is formed from the signifier 'arbor' and the concept 'tree'. The signifier and signified are intimately united, and call for each other, like the two sides of a coin – 'a concept is a quality of its phonic substance just as a particular slice of sound is a quality of the concept' (Saussure, p. 66). But the bond between signifier and signified is arbitrary.

> The idea of 'sister' is not linked by any inner relationship to the succession of sounds s-ö-r which serves as its signifier in French; that it could be represented equally by just any other sequence is proved by differences among languages and by the very existence of different languages: the signified 'Ox' has as its signifier b-ö-f on one side of the border and o-k-s (ochs) on the other (Saussure, pp. 67-8).

Turning to the linking of signs: Saussure emphasized the notion of value (valeur), the setting of the sign, the relation of the sign to other signs, its environment. More important than the quantity of phonic matter that a sign contains is what there is around it in the other signs. Thus

> Modern french mouton can have the same signification as english sheep but not the same value . . . particularly because in speaking of a piece of meat ready to be served on the table, english uses mutton and not sheep. The difference in value between sheep and mouton is due to the fact that sheep has beside it a second term while the french does not (Saussure, pp. 115-6).

La langue is a system of interdependent terms in which the value of each term results only from the simultaneous presence of the others. The value of any term is determined by its environment. What follows from this is that signs do not signify anything in themselves, but a sign marks a difference of meaning between itself and other signs. La langue is thus made up of differences. Meaning is diacritical, or differential, based on differences between terms, and not on intrinsic properties of the terms themselves.

In modern terminology morphemes are the smallest constituents of language that can carry a meaning. Phonemes are those sounds which are able to distinguish words – e.g., bed and bad are distinguished by the phonemes *a* and *e*. Each phoneme presupposes a network of oppositions with other phonemes of the language system. In addition, each phoneme is made up of a bundle of 'distinctive features'. Each distinctive feature involves a choice between 'two terms of an opposition that displays a specific differential property, divergent from the properties of all other oppositions' (Jakobson and Halle, p. 4) – e.g., voiced as opposed to unvoiced, consonantal/nonconsonantal, nasal/oral, etc. Thus the phoneme is actually a complex entity; it is not the phoneme but each of its distinctive features which is an irreducible and purely oppositive entity.

For Saussure, relations and differences between linguistic terms fall into two closely related groups or planes, which correspond to two forms of mental activity – syntagmatic and associative planes. The syntagm is a combination based on linearity.

In discourse, words acquire relations based on the linear nature of la langue because they are chained together. This rules out the possibility of pronouncing two elements simultaneously. The elements are arranged, in sequence on the chain of speech. The syntagm is always composed of two, or more consecutive units (e.g. french ré-lire, reread, contre tous, against everyone . . . etc.). In the syntagm a term acquires its value only because it stands in opposition to everything that precedes or follows it, or to both (Saussure, p. 123).

As for the associative plane, 'Outside discourse . . . words acquire relations of a different kind. Those that have something in common are associated in the memory resulting in groups marked by diverse relations' (Saussure, p. 123). Thus 'education' can be associated with many other words, through its meaning to training, upbringing, etc; or through its sound to educate, educator, applicator, etc. Thus the syntagmatic plane is more closely related to speech, and the associative plane to la langue.

Jakobson has adapted these two planes. He described how the development of a discourse may take place along two different semantic lines – it is called metaphoric when one topic leads to another through their similarity; or metonymic when one topic leads to another through their contiguity. In any discourse, both metaphoric and metonymic poles will be present, but one may dominate. Metaphor is related to similarity and to selection – 'A selection between alternatives implies the possibility of substituting one for another . . . selection and substitution are two faces of the same operation' (Jakobson and Halle, p. 60). This is like Saussure's associative plane. Metonymy is related to contiguity and combination, the combination of sign to sign in a context, and is like the syntagmatic plane. Lacan modified Jakobson's terms (see chapter 6) – he linked metonymy to the connection of word-to-word, and related this to the Freudian concept of displacement; and he linked metaphor to the replacement of one word for another, relating this to the Freudian concept of condensation.

Saussure's ideas, in particular, laid the foundation for modern structural linguistics. The term Structuralism when applied by subsequent thinkers to the various human sciences refers essentially to some basic dialogue with structural linguistics. Lévi-Strauss' work in anthropology is a prime example of the fertility of the linguistic model, and he was a major influence on Lacan. Lévi-Strauss wrote:

Structural linguistics shifts from the study of conscious linguistic phenomena to study of their unconscious infrastructure; it does not treat terms as independent entities, taking instead as its basis of analysis the relations between terms . . . it introduces the concept of system . . . [and it] aims at discovering general law (Lévi-Strauss, 1963, p. 33).

One studies not only what the terms have in common, what is universal; but also what differentiates them from each other, what is particular. Lévi-Strauss took this model for his work on the structure of myths and kinship systems, which he claimed are built by the mind on the level of unconscious thought. For him, the unconscious imposes structural laws upon basic inarticulated elements, such as emotions, memories and impulses.

The role of unconscious linguistic processes has a long history which begins before Freud. Saussure himself distinguished between the unconscious activity (l'activité inconsciente) of speakers and the conscious operations (opérations conscientes) of the linguist. The American anthropologist and linguist Boas wrote that 'the single sound as such has no independent existence . . . it never enters the consciousness of the speaker, but exists only as a part of a sound-complex which conveys a definite meaning' (1911, p. 19). Boas also discussed the relation between the unconscious character of linguistic phenomena and more conscious ethnological phenomena, work which greatly influenced Lévi-Strauss.

APPENDIX 2

BRIEF BIOGRAPHY
OF JACQUES LACAN

Born in Paris, 1901.

Medical training in the Paris Medical Faculty. Became Chef de Clinique in 1932.

Doctoral thesis for psychiatric degree – 'Paranoid psychosis and its relation to the personality' (1932).

Association with the French surrealist movement, from early 1930s.

1934 – Joined the Société Psychanalytique de Paris.

1936 – Presented paper on the 'mirror stage' to the International Psychoanalytic Congress in Marienbad.

Until 1952 – Distinguished member of the French psychoanalytic establishment. Intellectual contacts with Merleau-Ponty and Lévi-Strauss, through the Collège Philosophique, Paris.

1953 – Presentation of the Rome Discourse. Controversy within the Paris psychoanalytic society. Daniel Lagache, followed by Lacan, formed a new Société Française de Psychanalyse. Formation of Lacan's Seminar.

1953 to early 1960s – continuous development of ideas, particularly those put forward as programme in the Rome Discourse, involving psychoanalysis and linguistics.

1963 – Expelled, finally, from International Psychoanalytic Association, because of unorthodox practice and teaching methods.

1964 – Reformed his analytic society, calling it L'Ecole Freudienne de Paris.

———

1966 – Publication of his *Ecrits*, followed by explosion of his influence in French society. He soon became a cultural phenomenon.

1966 to 1980 – Increasing interest in his work in France and abroad.

1968 – May Revolution. Lacan supported the students' revolt. President of the psychoanalytic department of University of Vincennes.

1980 – Dissolved the Ecole Freudienne, and formed La Cause Freudienne. Expulsion of many previously close collaborators. Legal battles.

1981 – Death.

Bibliography

de Beauvoir, S. (1948) *The Second Sex*, trans. by Parshley, H.M., London, Jonathan Cape, 1953.

Benvenuto, S. (1984) *La strategia freudiana*, Naples, Liguori, S.r.l.

Bowie, M. (1979) 'Jacques Lacan', in Sturrock, John, ed., *Structuralism and Since*, Oxford, Oxford University Press, pp. 116-153.

Boas, F. (1911) 'Introduction to Handbook of American Indian Languages', in Holder, Preston, ed., *American Indian Languages*, Lincoln, University of Nebraska Press, 1966, pp. 1-79.

Brunswick, R. (1928) 'A Supplement to Freud's "History of an Infantile Neurosis"', *International Journal of Psychoanalysis* 9, pp. 439-449.

Clavreul, J. (1977) *L'Ordre médical*, Paris, Editions du Seuil.

Clément, C. (1981) *Vies et légendes de Jacques Lacan*, Paris, Editions G. Fasquelle.

Contri, G., ed. (1978) *Lacan in Italia/Lacan en Italie*, Milan, La Salamandra.

Deleuze, G. and Guattari, F. (1972) *L'Anti-oedipe*, Paris, Editions de Minuit.

Derrida, J. (1967) *Writing and Difference*, trans. by Bass, A., London, Routledge and Kegan Paul, 1978.

Freud, S. (1895) 'Project for a Scientific Psychology', London, Hogarth Press, 1954; Standard Ed., 1, pp. 283-392.

THE WORKS OF JACQUES LACAN

Freud, S. (1900) *The Interpretation of Dreams*, London, 1955; Standard Ed., 4-5.

—— (1901) *The Psychopathology of Everyday Life*, London, 1960; Standard Ed., 6.

—— (1905) *Jokes and their Relation to the Unconscious*, London, 1960; Standard Ed., 8.

—— (1909a) 'Analysis of a Phobia in a Five-Year-Old Boy', London, 1955; Standard Ed., 10, pp. 1-149.

—— (1909b) 'Notes upon a Case of Obsessional Neurosis', London, 1955; Standard Ed., 10, pp. 151-318.

—— (1911a) 'Formulations on the two Principles of Mental Functioning', London, 1958; Standard Ed., 12, pp. 213-226.

—— (1911b) 'Psychoanalytic Notes on an Autobiographical Account of a Case of Paranoia (Dementia Paranoides)', London, 1958; Standard Ed., 12, pp. 1-82.

—— (1914) 'On Narcissism: an Introduction', London, 1957; Standard Ed., 14, pp. 67-102.

—— (1918) 'From the History of an Infantile Neurosis', London, 1955; Standard Ed., 17, pp. 1-122.

—— (1920) *Beyond the Pleasure Principle*, London, 1955; Standard Ed., 18, pp. 1-64.

—— (1923) *The Ego and the Id*, London, 1961; Standard Ed., 19, pp. 1-66.

—— (1924) 'Neurosis and Psychosis', London, 1961; Standard Ed., pp. 147-153.

—— (1925) 'Negation', London, 1959; Standard Ed., 19, pp. 233-239.

—— (1926) *The Question of Lay Analysis*, London, 1947; Standard Ed., 20, pp. 179-258.

—— (1933) *New Introductory Lectures on Psychoanalysis*, London, 1964; Standard Ed., pp. 1-182.

Habermas, J. (1968) *Knowledge and Human Interests*, London, Heinemann.

Hegel, G.W.F. (1807) *Phenomenology of Spirit*, trans. by Miller, A.V., Oxford, Clarendon Press, 1977.

226

Heidegger, M. (1926) *Being and Time*, trans. by Macquarrie, J. and Robinson, E., Oxford, Basil Blackwell, 1962.

Irigaray, L. (1974) *Speculum de l'autre femme*, Paris, Editions de Minuit.

Jakobson, R. and Halle, M. (1956) *The Fundamentals of Language*, The Hague, Mouton.

Köhler, W. (1925) *The Mentality of Apes*, trans. by Winter, E., Harmondsworth, Penguin, 1957.

Lacan, J. (1931a) 'Structures des psychoses paranoiaques', *Semaine des Hôpitaux de Paris*, Juillet, pp. 437-445.

—— (1931b) 'Ecrits "Inspirés": schizographie', *Annales médico-psychologiques* 2, pp. 508-522.

—— (1932) *De la psychose paranoiaque dans ses rapports avec la personnalité*, Paris, Editions du Seuil, 1975.

—— (1935) 'Hallucinations et délire', *Evolution psychiatrique* 1, pp. 87-91.

—— (1936) 'Au delà du principe de réalité, *Evolution psychiatrique* 3, pp. 67-86.

—— (1938) 'La famille: le complexe, facteur concret de la pathologie familiale et les complexes familiaux en pathologie' in *Encyclopédie Française*, Paris, Larousse, 8, pp. 3-16.

—— (1947) 'La psychiatrie anglaise et la guerre', *Evolution Psychiatrique* 1, pp. 293-318.

—— (1949) 'Le stade du miroir comme formateur de la fonction du Je', *Revue française de psychanalyse* 4, pp. 449-455. Translated in *Ecrits* (1977) as 'The mirror stage as formative of the function of the I', pp. 1-7.

—— (1953a) 'Some Reflections on the Ego', *International Journal of Psycho-analysis* 34, pp. 11-17.

—— (1953b) 'Fonction et champ de la parole et du langage en psychanalyse (Rapport de Rome)', *La Psychanalyse* (1956) 1, pp. 81-166. Translated in *Ecrits* (1977) as 'The function and field of speech and language in psycho-analysis', pp. 30-113.

—— (1953-4) *Le séminaire 1: les écrits techniques de Freud*

(Freud's Technical Papers), Paris, Editions du Seuil, 1975.

—— (1954-5) *Le séminaire 2: le moi dans la théorie de Freud et dans la technique de la psychanalyse* (The Ego in Freudian Theory and Psychoanalytic Technique), Paris, Editions du Seuil, 1978.

—— (1955-6) *Le séminaire 3: les psychoses* (The Psychoses), Paris, Editions du Seuil, 1981.

—— (1956a) 'Réponse au commentaire de Jean Hyppolite sur la Verneinung de Freud', *La Psychanalyse* 1, pp. 17-28.

—— (1956b) 'Le séminaire sur "La lettre volée"', *La Psychanalyse* 2, pp. 1-44. Translated by Mehlman, J., *Yale French Studies* 48, 1972, pp. 38-72.

—— (1956-7) 'La relation d'objet et les structures freudiennes', (Summaries of Lacan's Seminar 1956-7). *Bulletin de Psychologie* (Paris) 10, pp. 426-430, 602-605, 742-743, 851-854; 11, pp. 31-34.

—— (1957) 'L'Instance de la lettre dans l'inconscient ou La Raison depuis Freud', *La Psychanalyse* 3, pp. 47-81. Translated in *Ecrits* (1977) as 'The agency of the letter in the unconscious or reason since Freud', pp. 146-178.

—— (1957-8) 'D'Une question préliminaire à tout traitement possible de la psychose', *La Psychanalyse* 4, pp. 1-50. Translated in *Ecrits* (1977) as 'On a question preliminary to any possible treatment of psychosis', pp. 179-225.

—— (1958) 'La signification du phallus', *Ecrits* (1966), pp. 685-695. Translated in *Ecrits* (1977) as 'The signification of the phallus', pp. 281-291.

—— (1960) 'Subversion du sujet et dialectique du désir dans l'inconscient freudien', *Ecrits* (1966), pp. 793-827. Translated in *Ecrits* (1977) as 'The subversion of the subject and the dialectic of desire in the Freudian unconscious', pp. 292-325.

—— (1964) *Le séminaire 11: les quatre concepts fondamentaux de la psychanalyse*, Paris, Editions du Seuil, 1973. *The Four Fundamental Concepts of Psychoanalysis*, trans. by Sheridan, A., Harmondsworth, Penguin, 1977.

—— (1966) *Ecrits*, Paris, Editions du Seuil. Of the above

essays cited in this bibiography, the following are included in the *Ecrits* (1966); Lacan, 1936, 1949, 1953b, 1956a, 1956b, 1957, 1957-8, 1958 and 1960.

—— (1972-3) *Le séminaire 20: Encore*, Paris, Editions du Seuil, 1975.

—— (1974) *Télévision*, Paris, Editions du Seuil.

—— (1982) *Annuaire et textes statutaires* (Statutes of La Cause, and Lacan's writings on the analytic institution), Paris, Editions Ecole de la Cause Freudienne.

Lacoue-Labarthe, P. and Nancy, J-L. (1973) *Le titre de la lettre*, Paris, Editions Galilée.

Laing, R.D. (1960) *The Divided Self*, London, Tavistock Publications.

Laplanche, J. and Pontalis, J-B. (1967) *The Language of Psychoanalysis*, trans. by Nicholson-Smith, D., London, Hogarth Press, 1973.

Leclaire, S. (1968) *Psychanalyser*, Paris, Editions de Minuit.

Leclaire, S. (1973) *On tue un enfant*, Paris, Editions du Seuil.

Lefort, R. and R. (1980) *Naissance de l'autre*, Paris, Editions du Seuil.

Lemaire, A. (1970) *Jacques Lacan*, trans. by Macey, D., London, Routledge and Kegan Paul, 1977.

Lemoine-Luccioni, E. (1976) *Partage des femmes*, Paris, Editions du Seuil.

Lévi-Strauss, C. (1958) *Structural Anthropology*, trans. by Jacobson, C. and Grundfest Schoepf, B., Harmondsworth, Penguin, 1968.

Locke, J. (1689) *An Essay Concerning Human Understanding*, ed. Nidditch, P.H., Oxford, Clarendon Press, 1975.

Mannoni, M. (1979) *La théorie comme fiction*, Paris, Editions du Seuil.

Mannoni, O. (1969) *Clefs pour l'imaginaire ou l'autre scène*, Paris, Editions du Seuil.

Mehlman, J. (1972) 'The "Floating Signifier": from Lévi-Strauss to Lacan', *Yale French Studies* 48, pp. 10-37.

Merleau-Ponty, M. (1945) *The Phenomenology of Perception*,

trans. by Smith, C., London, Routledge and Kegan Paul, 1962.

Merleau-Ponty, M. (1964) *The Visible and the Invisible*, trans. by Lingis, A., Evanston Illinois, Northwestern University Press, 1969.

Mitchell, J. (1974) *Psychoanalysis and Feminism*, Harmondsworth, Penguin.

Mitchell, J. and Rose, J. (1982) *Feminine Sexuality, Jacques Lacan and the école freudienne*, London, Macmillan.

Rosemont, F., ed. (1978) *What is Surrealism? Selected Writings of André Breton*, London, Pluto Press.

Plato (1951) *The Symposium*, trans. by Hamilton, W., Harmondsworth, Penguin.

Safouan, M. (1974) *Etudes sur l'oedipe*, Paris, Editions du Seuil.

Safouan, M. (1979) *L'échec du principe de plaisir*, Paris, Editions du Seuil.

Safouan, M. (1983) *Jacques Lacan et la question de la formation des analystes*, Paris, Editions du Seuil.

Sapir, E. (1921) *Language*, London, Rupert Hart-Davis, 1963.

Schneiderman, S. (1980) *Returning to Freud*, Yale, Yale University Press.

Schneiderman, S. (1983) *Jacques Lacan: the Death of an Intellectual Hero*, Harvard, Harvard University Press.

Schatzman, M. (1973) *Soul Murder*, Harmondsworth, Penguin.

Schreber, D.P. (1903) *Memoirs of My Nervous Illness*, trans. by Macalpine, I. and Hunter, R., London, Dawson and Sons, 1955.

Segal, H. (1979) *Klein*, London, Fontana.

Turkle, S. (1978) *Psychoanalytic Politics*, New York, Basic Books.

Wilden, A. (1968) *The Language of the Self*, Baltimore, Johns Hopkins Press.

Zeldin, T. (1980) *France: Intellect and Pride*, Oxford, Oxford University Press.

INDEX

133-5, 153, 158-9
Nancy, J-L., 106, 109, 116
narcissism, 49-50, 52, 59-60, 81, 98,
143, 190
natural science, 15, 20-1, 63-5, 109
need, 132, 174-5 (see demand and
desire)
neurology, 31
neurosis, 136, 143-4, 181; infantile
neurosis, 149; traumatic
neurosis, 91
neurosyphilis, 31

object relations, 126-30
objet a, 176-81, 187, 189
obsessional state, 143
Oedipus, 88-9
Oedipus complex, 25, 27, 125,
126-41, 161, 177-8, 195
ontology, 170, 172-4
Ornicar, 211
Other, 73, 86-7, 130, 146, 158,
169-70, 173, 178, 181, 193, 195,
208-10; barred Other, 175-6,
181; desire of, 130-2; field of,
129; locus of, 86-7, 159-60
other, 73, 86-7, 133, 186

paranoid-schizoid position, 127
part object, 127, 177, 179
pass, the, 206-8, 212
penis, 131, 136-7
perversions, 81, 132-6, 181
phallus, 130-6, 158-60, 177-81,
186-95
phenomenology, 68-71
philosophy, 15, 27, 62, 77, 107,
116, 165-6, 199-200, 202
phobia, 70; of 'little Hans', 25,
136-41

Plato, 179
pleasure (lust), 92, 152, 178-9,
187-91
Poe, E., 23-4, 90, 91-102
poetry, 107, 115-6, 119-20
Popper, K., 201
positive sciences, 20-1, 63, 165-6,
201
preconscious, 47-51
prematurity of birth, 54-5
primal scene, 94-5, 149-50
projection, 44, 127, 142
psychiatry, 19, 31-4, 46, 65
psychical phenomenon, 70
psychical reality, 66, 69
psychoanalysis: in France, 32,
205-13; and human sciences,
20-1; identity of, 104, 106; and
mathematics, 109; and other
disciplines, 15, 201; and science,
20-1, 63-5, 77-8; and university,
103-5
psychoanalysts, 22, 26, 71-4, 79,
88, 192, 196-213
psychoanalytic relationship, 62,
84-5, 92, 101, 169-70, 181-2, 183,
187
psychoanalytic training, 12, 14, 21,
78-80, 103-4, 196-213
psychology: object of, 64-70
psychosis, 25-6, 31-46, 49, 63, 81,
131, 135-6, 142-61, 169, 172
puns, 13

Rank, O., 204
reality principle, 20, 48, 60, 63-74
Real Order, 80-2, 144, 146, 148-9,
152-3, 159-60, 166, 186
reason, 14, 24, 103, 107
repetition compulsion, 91-3
repression, 92, 123-4, 151-3, 168
return to Freud, 10-12, 27, 196

This edition of
The Works of Jacques Lacan
An Introduction
was finished in April 1986

It was set in 10/12 Garamond
on a CRTronic 300 phototypesetter and
printed by a Harris cold-set web offset press
onto Publishers' Antique Wove
80 g/m², vol. 19 paper

The book was commissioned by Robert M. Young
edited by Ann Scott, designed by
Carlos Sapochnik and produced
by Free Association Books